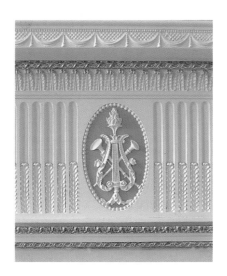

A Guide to the History
Architecture and Decoration of

DUFF HOUSE

Sponsored by Mobil
to celebrate the restoration of the house
and its opening as a country house museum
to display furniture and works of art drawn
from the collections of the National
Galleries of Scotland, Dunimarle
& the Marquess of Zetland

1995

IAN GOW AND
TIMOTHY CLIFFORD

Duff House

NATIONAL GALLERIES
OF SCOTLAND · EDINBURGH
MCMXCV

Published by the Trustees
of the National Galleries of Scotland
© the Trustees of the National Galleries
of Scotland 1995

ISBN 0 903598 55 8

Photography by Jack Mackenzie
Additional photography by Antonia Reeve
and from the collections of Bodie's of Banff,
Country Life, Historic Scotland, the Royal Commission
on the Ancient and Historical Monuments of Scotland
Designed and typeset by Dalrymple
Printed by Inglis Allen

Half title page
Detail of Apollo's Lyre, from the chimmeypiece
in the North Drawing Room

Frontispiece
Duff House by William Daniel
1822

Introduction

Empty houses, however architecturally distinguished, can be depressing and forlorn. So I found some ten years ago, when travelling along the coast road, the A98, and crossing the bridge over the River Deveron. I first set eyes on Duff House, sited close to the shores of the Moray Firth, surrounded by a golf-links midway between the small fishing burghs of Macduff and Banff. Duff House sits oddly and gloriously out of place, no distance from the extreme north-east tip of Scotland, a flamboyant classical palace beached in a seaside landscape.

Visitors will remember that even ten years ago Duff House was open to the public, but only two rooms had been decorated; there were four family portraits of the former owners on display, but otherwise it was populated by a scatter of cut-paper white mannequins, like ghosts, seated in the principal rooms. The portraits only added to the tragic sense of loss – not just of an aristocratic world, complete with its complement of butlers, housekeepers, footmen, ladies' maids, 'tweenies', cooks, parlour maids, and coachmen – but also its lack of estate workers centred around the great house – grieves, stewards, foresters, ploughmen, stockmen, gamekeepers, and estate carpenters and masons. This house, the most sophisticated eighteenth-century pile in northern Scotland, had once been a private treasure house, elegantly decorated with rich curtains, carpets, pictures, sculptures, a great library, and fine collections, particularly of historical portraits, prints, coins, and medals. Logs once burned in the fireplaces, bells rang below stairs for the servants, there were feasts, music, games and, above all, intense discussion about wars and politics, genealogy, agriculture, and even natural philosophy. Professor Alan Tait, in the only previous guidebook (*Duff House*, HMSO, 1985) lamented: '… the rich profusion of furnishings and paintings is beyond recall.' Not all of this atmosphere can be brought back, of course, but filling the house once more with appropriate furnishings and pictures can help us imagine more clearly the former function and spirit of a remarkable house.

It is not my purpose here to chronicle the vicissitudes of Duff House's history: the inspired choice of William Adam (1689–1748) as architect of the new house (1735–) commissioned by William Duff, Lord Braco (1697–1763); Adam's overcharging for the stonemasons' work, and Braco's subsequent fulminations and furious litigation; Braco's abandonment of completing the fitting-out of the interiors; the split loyalties between Braco and his Jacobite eldest son over the '45; the 2nd Earl of Fife's pioneering policy of collecting in Scotland historical portraits; the 4th Earl's glorious record fighting with Wellesley (later the 1st Duke of Wellington) in the Peninsular War; the 6th Earl of Fife's wedding at Buckingham Palace to HRH The Princess Louise, eldest daughter of the Prince of Wales (later King Edward VII), on 27 July 1889, and his creation as 1st Duke. The Fifes, in serious financial difficulties, then disposed of the house and 140 acres to the burgh of Banff in 1906, and it then suffered a very chequered history as a hospital and an hotel and, during the last War, as a POW camp and billet for Polish and Norwegian troops. In spite of its remote rural position, it was unlucky enough to have its sole pavilion bombed by the Luftwaffe in 1942.

Duff House was taken back into care in 1956 by the Secretary of State for Scotland, and was administered by a succession of bodies: the Ministry of Works, Scottish Development Department, and Historic Buildings and Monuments – what has now become Historic Scotland. Under the latter's direction a public meeting was called in 1988 to try to find a suitable future role for the house. Many bodies were then present, including the Scottish Office Education Department, the National Trust for Scotland, the National Museums of Scotland, Aberdeen

Museums & Art Galleries, Grampian Regional Council, Grampian Enterprise, the Scottish Tourist Board, and Banff & Buchan District Council.

Eventually, after a second meeting, the National Galleries of Scotland proposed that if running costs could be secured locally, and if the building were to be properly restored and suitably equipped for museum purposes, they would provide not only pictures for the house but also endeavour to find suitable furnishings. Under the auspices of Sir Hector Monro MP, the Minister for both Historic Scotland and the Scottish Office Education Department (Sponsor Department for the National Galleries of Scotland), an agreement in principle was signed on 21 July 1992 and then intensive meetings were set in train among the interested parties – Historic Scotland, the National Galleries of Scotland, Grampian Regional Council, Grampian Enterprise, and Banff & Buchan District Council.

By all these bodies pulling together with a belief in the house, it is now assured of an exciting future. The building, which has had Historic Scotland spend £2 million on the fabric, is now equipped with an excellent kitchen and restaurant, a shop, an audio-visual room, a lecture room, cloakrooms, a staff flat, and a new car park. Duff House has been entirely re-decorated, re-wired, re-plumbed, and equipped with the latest heat and smoke detectors, a sprinkler system, a lift, closed-circuit television, other security devices, and humidifiers. Grampian Regional Council and Banff & Buchan District Council have been responsible, amongst other things, for paying the running costs and for a full complement of staff – Manager, Secretary, Head Warder, warders, and cleaners. It is reassuring that so much has been achieved in so short a time by a group so disparate and so widely spread geographically. All have co-operated closely in this enterprise, and we now hope that Duff House itself will play its part in attracting the public to visit this architectural gem.

Historic Scotland have been responsible for the fabric, with the decoration under the control of Rab Snowden and the Stenhouse Conservation Centre. They have meticulously recorded the various layers of the house's decoration; that has been undertaken at the same time as major archival research, and the results have been transcribed by Dr Edward M. Furgol. Without this information, Ian Gow of the Royal Commission on the Ancient and Historical Monuments of Scotland could not have compiled this publication. The National Galleries of Scotland drew up the specifications for the warding, mechanical security, and the special requirements of a museum climate, including blinds and ultra-violet filters. They then sought out, mostly from their own reserves, nearly all the pictures now hanging at Duff House. The pictures have not been chosen for their 'star' quality – although there are many stars amongst them – but to furnish appropriately a great aristocratic Scottish country house. We make no apology for the preponderance of portraits, because that is what has always hung here. We also make no apology for the dense picture-hanging arrangements, for this again closely follows the pattern of how the house must have looked in its heyday.

The National Galleries of Scotland have no responsibility for looking after the applied arts – that is, furniture, metalwork, ceramics, glass, textiles, and enamels; they have, therefore, sought out this material largely on loan and have been remarkably fortunate. Most of the furnishings have been supplied on a twenty-five year loan from the Magdalene Sharpe Erskine Trust of Dunimarle, Culross, Fife – sometimes described as the Erskine of Torrie Institute. The Sharpe Erskine Collection not only contains a very handsome run of Erskine family portraits, stretching back to the seventeenth century, but also a fine collection of Old Master paintings (principally Dutch) and some very rich and splendid Napoleonic furniture.

This collection was the subject of a remarkable, fully-illustrated, manuscript catalogue compiled in 1910–12 by its third Curator (and Chaplain to the Episcopalian chapel of St Serf's), the Reverend James Harper, Canon of St Ninian's Cathedral, Perth. From Harper's introduction we learn that Dunimarle was bought in 1835 for £5,000 by Miss Magdalene Erskine, and that after settling there she 'became the wife of Admiral Sharpe, and bore henceforth the name of Mrs Sharpe Erskine … the romantic old lady in her senescence married one who had been an early lover – a union which lasted exactly three days and terminated in permanent separation.'

Mrs Sharpe Erskine died at the age of 85 on

1 February 1872, and by her Will all her property was left to Trustees for the purpose of founding and maintaining 'an Institution for the promotion of the study of the Fine Arts – the collection of paintings and other vertû made by herself and her brothers, Sir James and Sir John Erskine, being made the commencement of a fine Art Gallery.' This remarkable assemblage included Mrs Sharpe Erskine's own collection and those of her brothers and father. The family pictures all came from Torrie, nearby, while the majority of Old Masters were bequeathed to Edinburgh University by her brother, Sir James, a Major-General in the Peninsular War under Wellesley (later the 1st Duke of Wellington) and for very many years were displayed by the National Galleries of Scotland. Most are now on show at the Talbot Rice Gallery, University of Edinburgh, while many of his bronzes and finest hardstone vases are on loan to the National Galleries of Scotland in Edinburgh. The pictures that were in Sir James Erskine's London home formed part of the Dunimarle Collection, as did – according to Canon Harper – 'a good deal of the finest furniture, including the Napoleonic suites … He was with the Duke of Wellington at the debâcle of Napoleon and he had opportunities of acquiring Empire furniture. But he seems to have paid royally for it.'

The National Galleries of Scotland have also been most fortunate to have been lent by the Marquess of Zetland (head of the Dundas Clan) a very handsome suite of Neilson tapestries, designed by François Boucher and originally at Moor Park, Hertfordshire. This is a most appropriate loan, for another suite used to belong to the Fifes and was kept in Fife House, London. The Zetlands have also lent some of a very grand suite of seat furniture made for Sir Lawrence Dundas, for his London mansion in Arlington Street, by Thomas Chippendale to the design of Robert Adam; again, this is most appropriate as Robert was the most celebrated son of the architect of Duff House, William Adam. A single chair from this suite is in the Victoria and Albert Museum.

These are early days, but it is intended to complete the furnishing of all of Duff House's rooms with curtains and carpets. It is also intended to provide the Public with a definitive list of the contents on display. The National Galleries of Scotland through their Sponsor Department, the Scottish Office Education Department, have also been provided with limited monies to buy special furniture, making prudent use of end-of-year unspent balances. With the combination now of National Galleries of Scotland furniture and pictures, and the loans from Dunimarle and the Marquess of Zetland, we have endeavoured to furnish the house, appropriately guided but not inhibited by the original function of the rooms. Visitors should be assured that, even though the furnishing of the house may be incomplete, there is now an exciting future for this noble architectural masterpiece. Much of the lost spirit of Duff House has been revived by infusions from other, appropriately ancient and distinguished Scottish collections.

Finally, we are most grateful to Mobil North Sea Limited for their generous support which has enabled us to produce a guidebook worthy of this great house.

TIMOTHY CLIFFORD
Director, National Galleries of Scotland
April 1995

Many of the rooms still require carpets, curtains, and other fittings appropriate for the various different rooms' specific functions. We hope to achieve this with the assistance of public companies and private individuals sponsoring a room by adoption. Details of these arrangements, which will provide suitable acknowledgement and special privileges for the sponsor or donor, may be obtained from the Director's Office at the National Galleries of Scotland in Edinburgh or from the Manager at Duff House.

A Tour of the Interior of Duff House

TIMOTHY CLIFFORD

THE VESTIBULE is arranged and hung broadly on the basis of three surviving late 19th-century photographs by an unknown photographer, of which the glass negatives now belong to Bodie's of Banff, that show the west, north, and east walls. It had become a curiously exotic room, with a compromise between the elaborate rococo plasterwork of the ceiling, the carved gilt-wood rococo looking-glass over the chimneypiece crowned by an eagle with outspread wings *c.*1760, and the neo-classical colour scheme of rose and grey, devised with acanthus *rinceaux* by John Jackson in 1814. Halls are more often than not austere and formal, but this clearly was not, at any rate by the 19th century, and functioned as a delightfully cluttered and informal drawing-room.

The spirit of the original picture arrangement has been copied, but with full-lengths by Mytens and Jamesone on the north wall to replace the two female full-lengths that hung there in the Fifes' day. The Daniel Mytens portrait of *George Hay, 1st Earl of Kinnoull,* signed and dated 1633, is on loan from the present Earl of Kinnoull. The portrait by Jamesone of *Anne Erskine, Countess of Rothes, with Lady Margaret Leslie and Lady Mary Leslie,* is signed and dated 1626. There is also a handsome group of portraits by Scougall, and on the west wall a great masterpiece by William Etty, *The Combat, Woman Pleading for the Vanquished – an ideal groupe.* This, according to Etty, was designed to symbolise the Beauty of Mercy. Exhibited at the Royal Academy in 1825, it was bought by Etty's friend, the painter John Martin, who sold it to the Scottish Academy in 1831, from where it passed to the National Gallery of Scotland. Amongst other notable portraits is one by Sir Joshua Reynolds of *Sir William Forbes of Pitsligo (1739–1806),* banker and author. To the right of the front door is a porter's chair covered in black horsehair, hooded to protect the occupant from draughts. It was recently bought from the collection of Sir John Howard-Lawson, Bart., of Corby Castle, Cumberland. Weapons were always appropriate and practical fittings-out for a hall. Sadly, we lack the '2 Stand of Colours – Banffshire Volunteers' that were placed here for convenience and listed in the 1809 inventory but, after conservation, trophies of arms from Dunimarle are destined for this room.

Anne, Countess of Rothes and her Daughters by George Jamesone 1626

The Vestibule looking East

Opposite
Detail of Victorian pier glass on west wall of the Dining Room

Following pages
The Vestibule looking west showing *The Combat* by William Etty

9

The pair of sofas standing against the north wall, covered with cherry red velvet and with tapered gilded legs ornamented with money moulding, are similar to others designed by Joseph Bonomi for Lambton Hall in 1800. They were originally in the State Drawing Room at Dunimarle. The granite-topped table beneath the Etty oil is also from Dunimarle, as are the two marble busts on granite columns by Thomas Campbell (1791–1858) of Major-General Sir James Erskine, Bart. (1772–1825) dated Rome 1823, and of his brother, Sir John Drummond Erskine, Bart. (1776–1836) dated 1836. The handsome carved gilt-wood chandelier is English, probably *c*.1730, and still is equipped with *Sinumbra* oil-lamp fittings *c*.1820. It comes from Dunimarle, where it hung on the stairs.

Marble bust of *Major-General Sir James Erskine of Torrie* by Thomas Campbell

The Vestibule leads straight through to the **Dining Room**, which is set out, as its function implies, with a late-18th century D-ended mahogany dining-table from Dunimarle, twenty mahogany ladder-backed dining-chairs in the 18th-century taste (but not period) with chequered linen seats. The gilt-bronze *tazza* in the centre of the table was made in Paris *c*.1815, probably by Pierre Philippe Thomire or one of his competitors, and is from Dunimarle. The pair of magnificent gilt-bronze nine-branched candelabra are after a design by C. H. Tatham (1801) and were made by Storr & Mortimer for the 4th Earl of Fife; they are on loan from a private collector. The chandelier is a modern copy of an 18th-century original, the mahogany tables carved with masks are Irish, and the pair of circular tiered 'dumb waiters' are *c*.1800 and again come from Dunimarle, as does the dinner service which is sometimes set out on the table.

Mrs Daniel Cunyngham by Allan Ramsay

On one table stands a tureen in the form of a boar's head, *c*.1750-54, of Strasbourg faïence (tin-glazed earthenware, factory of Paul Hannong), while on another stands a mahogany vase-shaped knife urn, English, *c*.1780. The richly carved and gilded candle sconces on the west wall are English, *c*. 1725, and are *en suite* with a pair at Belhus, Essex. These may be by James Richards, master carver to the Crown. The round looking-glasses in gilt-wood frames carved with masks of Ceres and Bacchus are English, *c*.1730.

Boar's head soup tureen in the Dining Room

Opposite The Dining Room

The *Dining Room* is hung with portraits by Allan Ramsay (1713–84) and his contemporaries, while Nasmyth's copy of Ramsay's *Self Portrait* also hangs here. Probably the finest picture is Ramsay's early full-length portrait of *Elizabeth, Mrs Daniel Cunyngham* in its magnificent original rococo frame, removed from storage in Edinburgh and specially cleaned and restored to be hung at Duff. The companion full-length portrait is a copy of an oil by Francis Cotes (1726–70) of the *2nd Earl of Fife (1729–1809)*. The original, painted in 1765, is now in the North Carolina Museum of Art, Raleigh; it had been sold

Marble bust of *William Adam* by an unknown artist

The chimneypiece in the Private Drawing Room

Opposite
The Private Drawing Room showing the portrait of *George II* by John Shackleton

by the Princess Royal at Christie's in July 1924. The 2nd Earl inherited Duff House from his father, and amassed a major collection of historical portraits. The majority of his collection was sold by his heirs at Christie's on 7 June 1907, in 146 lots. Appropriately for a dining room, over the chimneypiece hangs *A Toper*, perhaps painted to represent the sense of 'taste', by Alexis Grimou (*c.*1680–1740).

To the left is the **Private Drawing Room,** and on the east wall hang landscapes by or attributed to the Welsh artist, Richard Wilson (1714–82), who is not to be confused with the Scots landscapist, Andrew Wilson. One shows *A View in Italy* and the other *A View of Wilton House from the South-East*, and both come from Dunimarle. Sir James Erskine lent two Italian landscapes by Richard Wilson to the Edinburgh Institution in 1819 (Nos 2 and 87). The room is hung with Andrea Soldi's portrait of the Aberdeen architect, *James Gibbs,* who had built Balvenie Castle in 1724 for William Duff, but was not employed by him for Duff House. Over the chimneypiece is a *View of Loch Katrine* in a rich frame with broken entablature designed by William Adam for the parlour at Lawers, Perthshire, built *c.*1728 for General Sir James Campbell, brother-in-law of Adam's major patron, the Earl of Stair. A portrait of the General by William Aikman (1682–1731) hangs nearby. The mahogany tripod tea-table is British, *c.*1730, and the tripod pole-screen standing beside the chimneypiece has its original tent stitch needlework screen, and dates from *c.*1760. The room is dominated by a gilded table, consisting of addorsed and entwined dolphins from Dunimarle with a *pietra dura* top, while between the windows stands a carved mahogany pedestal, *c.*1760, on which stands an anonymous marble bust of the architect, William Adam. Nearby in a fine rococo frame, hangs a portrait of *James Duff of Corsindae (1678–1762)*, signed and dated 1760 by Cosmo Alexander of Aberdeen. James Duff, a cousin of William Duff, Lord Braco, was factor on Braco's Echt estate. On the west wall hangs, most appropriately, a full-length portrait of *King George II* by John Shackleton (d.1767), the monarch who raised William Duff to the peerage. The Fifes used to hang their portrait of the King in the *Vestibule.*

This room leads to the **Closet off the Private Drawing Room,** a blue room with black stencils, based loosely on the original scheme of 1814 by Jackson. Here is a series of engravings by Luigi Rossini (1790–1857), very much in the Piranesi manner, of views of Rome. The theme is the Grand Tour, and this little room now contains red-figured Apulian pottery, fragments of antique sculpture, a gouache, *View of the Bay of Naples*, and a delightful oil sketch of *Vesuvius in Eruption*. Here also is an Antique Roman marble torso. These are all from the collections at Dunimarle and perfectly represent the

Adoration of the Shepherds
Flemish, 15th century

Victorian mirrored door in the Prince of Wales's Bedroom

St Jerome in Penitence by El Greco *c*.1595

Opposite
The Prince of Wales's Bedroom

sort of objects brought back from Italy by Scottish gentlemen on the Grand Tour.

THE PRINCE OF WALES'S BEDROOM leads off the *Vestibule* to the right of the front door as one looks to the south; it was used by HM King Edward VII when Prince of Wales. His eldest daughter, HRH Princess Louise, married the 6th Earl of Fife. The bedroom is suitably grand, with a large, gilded four-poster bed hung in pink damask bought from The Drum, Edinburgh, and a dominant portrait of a member of the Spinola family from Genoa, attributed to Sir Anthony van Dyck (1599–1641); nearby is a portrait bust of Queen Victoria, the Prince's mother. The set of four gilt chairs, in the manner of Morel and Hughes, probably date from the 1820s. The rosewood table, *c.* 1815, at the foot of the bed is by James Mein (1759–1830) of Roxburgh Street and Butcher Market, Kelso, and the mahogany card-table between the windows is probably by William Trotter of Edinburgh, *c.*1810. A group of old master paintings hangs on the north wall, the most notable being the *tondo* of *The Madonna and Child with St John*, perhaps by Francesco Botticini (*c.*1446-97).

Leading off this room to the west is the ANTIQUARIAN CLOSET, containing a portrait by Sir Francis Grant (1803–78) of *Sir Walter Scott*, that arch antiquary, over the chimneypiece, and cabinets filled with antiquities and curiosities of natural history from the Dunimarle Collection (all items are individually labelled). The arm-chair with the armorial in a lozenge, partly seventeenth century, comes from Panmure House, Carnoustie. The companion chair with a crown on the cresting comes from Dunimarle, where it was believed to have belonged to Mary, Queen of Scots. It is, however, late-17th Century and is more likely to have been associated with Queen Mary (Stewart), wife of William of Orange.

If we return to the *Vestibule* and turn left by the front door, we enter *Lord MacDuff's Dressing Room,* which after 1857 was used as COUNTESS AGNES'S BOUDOIR. This, according to a photograph *c.*1870, was something of a little treasure room: the chimneypiece was surmounted by a gilt rococo looking-glass, *c.*1760, embellished with 'ho ho' birds on the cresting; tables were covered with small easel-like frames, studded with family miniatures; and the east wall was dominated by the Fife family's treasured painting 'Murillo's' *Seated Christ Child.* Some of the spirit is now retained by a good, old (although not period) rococo looking-glass, with El Greco's *St Jerome in Penitence* hanging in place of the Murillo and surrounded by old master oil paintings from the National Gallery of Scotland. On the west wall are two sections of a large dismembered painting on panel attributed to J. G. Cuyp (1594–1652). In a display case, adapted from the design of Adam Weisweiller (a cabinet-maker

Above Two fragments from a *Dutch Family Group* by Jacob Cuyp

Right Countess Agnes's Boudoir

much employed by Marie Antoinette), are a scatter of miniatures from Dunimarle. The room is furnished suitably for a boudoir, including a handsome Dutch, late-18th Century, tambour-fronted table standing between the windows, a rosewood brass-inlayed 'loo' table (English, *c.*1810), and a set of six sabre-legged chairs (English or Scottish, *c.*1810). The Chesterfield sofas covered with chintz are faithful reproductions of originals of *c.*1860.

The rather plain rectangular gilt-framed looking-glass between the windows bears the maker's label within an oval wreath 'Jackson / Essex Bridge / Dublin'. The firm was founded by Thomas Jackson in the 1740s, but this must apply to Richard Jackson of 5 Essex Bridge; Jackson's bills are to be found amongst the Conolly acounts at Castletown.

Leading off *Countess Agnes's Boudoir* is the CHINA CLOSET, filled with porcelain and pottery that belonged to Mrs Magdalene Sharpe Erskine (1781–1872) of Dunimarle, whose posthumous portrait hangs over the chimneypiece. The ceramics, of considerable interest and quality, are individually labelled.

Tucked to the north of this room is the *Family Bedchamber,* later called the HUNTING ROOM. The room now contains a suite of Louis XV-style gilt wood chairs and a sofa, all covered in Gobelins tapestry. Over the chimneypiece is a gilt wood mirror from Dunimarle, and many of the pictures either come from Dunimarle or the Mrs Gordon Fyfe gift to the Scottish National Portrait

Gallery. The room is dominated by the group portrait of *Sir William Erskine, 1st Baronet of Torrie, and his Family*, painted by David Allan in 1788. It represents: Sir William Erskine, 1st Baronet; his wife, Frances Erskine; William Erskine, 2nd Baronet; James Erskine, 3rd Baronet; John Drummond Erskine, 4th Baronet; and their sisters Frances, Henrietta, Elizabeth, and Magdalene (the benefactress of Dunimarle). David Allan (1744–96) was much admired by Sir William, for whom he also painted *A Highland Wedding at Blair Atholl* (1780) a celebrated picture which for many years has been on loan to the National Gallery of Scotland.

The chimneypiece in the Hunting Room

This in turn leads to what in 1761 was fitted up in red printed cotton as LADY MACDUFF'S DRESSING ROOM. It now contains portraits of women and children and some elegant Scottish furniture – the large mahogany Pembroke table with tassel toes dates from *c*.1765 and was probably made in Edinburgh. The finest piece of furniture in the room is the curious combined dressing-table, desk and chest of drawers, in mahogany, *c*. 1750, and probably Scottish. Another, similar and believed to be Irish, is in the Noel Terry Collection, Fairfax House, York.

Next to this dressing rooom is LADY MACDUFF'S CLOSET, now the ORIENTAL CLOSET, filled with Chinese and Japanese art and artefacts. The Windsor chair is made of yew and elm in the Gothic taste, and is of a type in fashion *c*.1765–1800. Others, very similar, are in the Victoria and Albert Museum.

Sir William Erskine of Torrie with his Family by David Allan 1788

Returning to the *Vestibule* via the *Family Bedchamber*, we cross, using the north-west door, to the GREAT STAIRCASE. The colour scheme of buffs and greys with fictive mouldings and bands of *rinceaux* ornament was, like the *Vestibule*, the work of John Jackson, 1814. By 1807 the *Staircase* was densely hung with 34 paintings, including copies after Snyders and Rubens from originals formerly in the Orléans Collection. Now it is hung with a full-size copy of Raphael's *Transfiguration* by Grigor Urquhart of Inverness (*c*.1797 – after 1846), painted *c*.1826, the original of which is now in the Vatican. Another enormous picture is the portrait of *Field-Marshal George, Marquess of Tweeddale (1787–1876)* in uniform and mounted on a horse. Originally on the stairs of Yester House, East Lothian, it was painted by Sir Henry Raeburn (1756–1823) and completed by his pupil, Colvin Smith (1795–1875). Dominating the foot of the stairs is the full-length portrait of *Mrs James Mackenzie* by Sir Daniel Macnee (1806-82). The Duff staircase is otherwise hung principally with Scottish portraits.

The Great Staircase

Standing at the bottom of the staircase is a monumental porphyry lion's paw supporting a *verde antico* marble basin or laver, the whole mounted on

a stepped plinth of polished black Parrot coal. It was previously at Torrie House, where it served as a wine cooler. This remarkable object is in part a restored ancient Roman fragment of the 1st or 2nd century A.D. Behind it is an intriguing case of stuffed Argus Pheasant, a Golden Pheasant, and two hen pheasants, which has the trade label of the London taxidermist on the back – *T Hall … City Row, Finsbury Square,* and is also dated *June 30, 1805.* These birds, pets of Mrs Magdalene Sharpe Erskine, come from Dunimarle. Around the walls are distributed a set of eight early-19th century chairs, with richly-carved backs with auricular Mannerist designs incorporating double-headed eagles, lions, monster masks, and putti. The set comes from Dunimarle and in the 1875 inventory was described as 'believed to have been the work of Albert Durer'. This sort of seat furniture, with fleshy auricular forms, derives from 17th century German prototypes in the manner of Friedrich Unteutsch (b. Berlin *c.*1600, working Frankfurt –1670), but continued to be made in the Tyrol well into the 19th century – not so much as a conscious revival of an ancient source, but what became the continuation of a local vernacular tradition. Standing on the table at the bottom of the stairs is a pair of large jars with covers, which are Japanese (Imari, *c.*1700–1720) and come from Dunimarle. At the top of the staircase is the **Marble Lobby**, painted with simulated Siena marble walls, faithfully copying a rich scheme devised for the 5th Earl in the 1860s. The niche contained a marble Venus after Giambologna (Giovanni da Bologna, 1529–1608) but now contains a bronzed plaster figure of a Vestal holding aloft a lamp in the manner of Humphrey Hopper (1767–1834). The *Marble Lobby* has now been used to display a series of historic plaster busts after the Antique, made by Carlo and Filippo Albacini in the 18th century and bought directly from the Albacini heirs in 1839 by the Scottish landscape painter, Andrew Wilson, for the Trustees' Academy of Edinburgh. Other busts from the same source are displayed on the north and south staircases at the National Gallery of Scotland, Edinburgh, and in the library at Paxton House, Berwickshire. The austere D-shaped table is probably French, *c.*1800, and is from Dunimarle. The handsome brass four-burner gasolier, of colza lamp form, is English *c.*1820–25. Closely-similar examples are in England at Nostell Priory, near Wakefield, and at Temple Newsam House, Leeds.

We enter the **North Drawing Room** by the door to the left of the niche. This room, like two other rooms in the house, may once have functioned as a dining-room but above all it served as a picture-gallery. It is now furnished as a drawing-room, and the picture arrangements loosely follow those of the room as it appears in two photographs of about 1870. The room had been

The Great Staircase showing the porphyry lion's paw supporting a marble basin

The Marble Lobby

Opposite The North Drawing Room

Detail from the chimneypiece in the North Drawing Room

Detail of the cornice in the North Drawing Room

Detail from the chimneypiece in the North Drawing Room

extensively re-furnished after 1857 by Countess Agnes, with the emphasis on comfort. The composition chimneypiece with the central oval tablet of a boar hunt in the forests of Calydon, taken from a Roman Meleager sarcophagus, dates from the late–18th Century and was bought in London. The corner blocks, with images of Polyhymnia and Thalia, Muses, respectively, of sublime hymn and comedy or idyllic poetry, are taken from the celebrated Muses' Sarcophagus then in the Capitoline Museum but now in the Louvre. These are separated by medallions of Apollo's lyre and crossed shepherd's-pipes, which provide an ornamental ensemble most appropriate for an 18th century Scottish nobleman's country drawing-room. The very large carved gilt pier glass over the chimneypiece dates from the 1860s, and is the only surviving piece of furniture dating from the Fifes' occupation of the house.

Opposite the pier glass hangs a large full-length copy by F. R. Pickersgill (1820–1900) of a portrait by Sir Henry Raeburn of *James, the 4th Earl of Fife*, (1776–1857), hero of the Peninsular War. He volunteered his services and attained the rank of Major-General in the Spanish Patriotic Army. He was wounded at Talavera and at the storming of Fort Matagorda near Cadiz. His pair of gilt-bronze candelabra are downstairs in the *Dining Room*. Around the walls hang a fine group of works by Raeburn (including the full-length portrait of *Lady Hume Campbell of Marchmont and Child*) and his contemporaries, as well as a selection of European old master paintings from Dunimarle, including works by or attributed to Backhuysen, Bourdon, Both, Hobbema, Ruysdael, Teniers, van der Neer, and Wouwermans.

Most are in handsome Empire-style frames, several with framemakers' labels from Edinburgh. They all belonged to Major-General Sir James Erskine (1772–1825) and were hung in his London house. As a Lieutenant-Colonel he commanded the 2nd Regiment of Dragoon Guards in the Peninsular War under Wellesley (later 1st Duke of Wellington), and married Lady Louisa Paget, daughter of the 1st Earl of Uxbridge; her brother, later the 1st Marquess of Anglesey, lost his leg at Waterloo.

Sir James Erskine was a keen connoisseur of old masters, and the bulk of his collection, which for many years hung at the National Gallery of Scotland, Edinburgh, is now mostly on display in the Talbot Rice Gallery, University of Edinburgh. He bought heavily in Paris in 1816, and continued to collect right up to the end of his life. Sir James was a founder director in 1819 of the Edinburgh Institute for 'the Encouragement of the Fine Arts in Scotland', and according to invoices at Dunimarle he acquired much of his picture collection through Pizzette of 16 Foley Place, London. He bought the pictures attributed to Teniers and Both from J. B. Pascal of Berlin on 7 January 1820, paying 1300 Prussian dollars, and Pignone's *Sta Prasseda* (then called *Dolce* and now sold) from Siegfried Bendixen at Hamburg on 13 August 1822 for 50 Frédérics d'Or. Immediately after Sir James's death in 1825, the collection was the subject of a valuation by the great scholar / dealer, Samuel Woodburn, who also handled Sir Thomas Lawrence's collection.

An arm-chair from Cardinal Fesch's suite

Much of the gilded furniture in this room was collected by Sir James Erskine and formerly fitted out the State Drawing Room or Napoleon Room at Dunimarle. It was all bought in Paris, and Sir James had to pay Customs charges on them at the rate of 60% of their declared value. The garniture of different Empire suites consists of two large arm-chairs with acanthus tailed griffins on the arms, six smaller chairs with pediment backs and winged lion arms, and eight others without arms *en suite*. Bought at the same time are the six Ottoman folding gilt stools (so-called 'tabouret en x') which are now in the *Great* or *South Drawing Room*.

There is confusion about these magnificent suites of furniture; one set, which originally consisted of at least thirty-six pieces, was made by Fratelli Santi, Rome, *c.*1800 (based on a drawing in the Cooper-Hewitt Museum, New York) and were said to have been given by Napoleon to his step-uncle, Cardinal Fesch (1763–1839), Archbishop of Paris and Lyons. They were in the Fesch Sale in Paris in 1816, and some were bought by Sir James, others (now in the Royal Pavilion, Brighton) by his cousin, Colonel James Moray, or his brother, William Moray of Abercairny, near Crieff, Perthshire, and still others descended to the Duke of Atholl, probably through his other cousins, the Drummond-Morays, and are now on loan to Beningborough Hall, North Yorkshire. A further group is at the Lady Lever Art Gallery, Port Sunlight.

Detail of the acanthus tailed griffin on one of the Fesch arm-chairs

The set with pedimented backs is French, like others at Malmaison, and corresponds, even to the colour of the upholstery, to a set once in the Grand Drawing Room of Beckford's Fonthill Abbey, Wiltshire, engraved in John Rutter's *Delineations of Fonthill*, Shaftesbury 1823, and the set of six stools at Fonthill also correspond. Some of the Dunimarle stools have been noted to bear the mark of the restored French Royal Family and the stamp for items from the Tuileries Palace. All of these remarkable pieces of furniture require conservation and deserve further research. What is specially unusual is that many of the chairs are still equipped with their original case covers in blue linen damask with crimson piping. The much more modest set of 14 painted beech chairs with rush seats are English, probably ordered by Jonas Brooke just before he died in 1784, and they come from Mere Hall, Knutsford, Cheshire.

From the *Marble Lobby*, we cross to the **GREAT** or **SOUTH DRAWING ROOM**.

Detail of a border from one of the Moor Park tapestries

L'aimable pastorale by François Boucher

Opposite The Great Drawing Room

The architectural decoration is very simple and austere, with a composition chimneypiece supplied from London, the central tablet depicting the *Triumph of Mars*. This sort of chimneypiece has its close counterpart at Leith Hall nearby (National Trust for Scotland). Within the fireplace stands a handsome pair of ormolu firedogs (or *chenets*) from Dunimarle, with gilded sphinxes back-to-back with flaming tripods (or *Athèniennes*). They are after the design of the architect, F. J. Bélanger, and possibly by Pitoin, *c.*1784/5. The walls are hung with some of a splendid suite of Gobelins tapestries from the workshop of Jacques Neilson (1714–88), with the reserves designed by François Boucher (1703–70) hanging like simulated framed paintings against grey damask walls. The decorative sections with flowers and birds (so-called *alentours*) were designed by Maurice Jacques (1712–84). These tapestries are on loan from the Marquess of Zetland, and were commissioned by Sir Lawrence Dundas in 1766 to hang at his English country house, Moor Park, Hertfordshire. Other, similar sets were commissioned, often through the agency of Robert Adam (William's son), for: Croome Park, Worcestershire (now in the Metropolitan Museum, New York); Newby Hall, Yorkshire; Weston Park, Shropshire; and Osterley Park, Middlesex (the National Trust). A set of Gobelins tapestries was at Fife House, London, so this is an especially appropriate loan. Sadly, it has not been possible to accommodate on display all the tapestries in this suite.

Particularly interesting are the *Pastorales* by François Boucher (1703–1770), the French rococo painter. In the eighteenth century they belonged to Louis-René, Marchal de Saincy, économe général du Clergé (an office of state changed with the taxation of the clergy), whose collection was dispersed in 1789. He also owned Boucher's great *Rising* and *Setting of the Sun* now in the Wallace Collection. The three *Pastorales* would have been hung as *trumeaux* (i.e. between the windows) in his Parisian hôtel just off the Place des Victoires. The paintings were acquired in the early nineteenth century by Baron Meyer Amschel Rothschild and hung at Mentmore.

Around the walls stand part of one of the very finest sets of British seat furniture. These two arm-chairs and two sofas, in gilded beech and walnut upholstered in crimson damask, were made by Thomas Chippendale (1718–79) to the design of Robert Adam (1728–92). They were supplied to Sir Lawrence Dundas for his London house in Arlington Street. The invoice reads: '9 July 1765 : 8 large Arm Chairs exceeding Richly Carv'd in the Antick manner and Gilt in oil Gold stuff'd and cover'd with your own Damask … and strong castors on the feet … 4 large Sofas exceeding Rich to match the chairs … [total] £510–4-0.' This included crimson check case-covers and leather outer covers. They were to the design of Robert Adam, who was paid in 1764 for a 'Design

Detail from the chimneypiece in the Great Drawing Room

Detail of the carved dolphin table in the Great Drawing Room

Gilded beech furniture made by Thomas Chippendale to the design of Robert Adam

of Sopha and Chairs for the Salon', and this drawing still survives in the Soane Museum, London.

This seat furniture, familiar to those who visited the *Treasure Houses of Britain* Exhibition at the National Gallery of Art, Washington D.C., in 1985/6, marks the sole occasion on which Chippendale is definitely known to have executed one of Adam's designs and, per chair, these cost almost twice as much as Chippendale ever charged in his long career, which gives some indication of their special quality. The set is kindly loaned, like the tapestries, by the Marquess of Zetland. Lord Zetland's ancestor Sir Lawrence Dundas, who commissioned the tapestries and furniture, was a merchant and contractor who made a fortune as Commissar-General of the Army in Scotland, Flanders, and Germany, and was then a Governor of the Bank of England from 1764 to 1777. His wealth was partly spent on improvements by Robert Adam to his London house at 19 Arlington Street and on his home in Edinburgh, built by Chambers in St Andrew Square (now the Royal Bank of Scotland).

The pair of gilt-wood candle-stands from Dunimarle date from *c*.1700–10, and are much in the manner of the designer Daniel Marot, who worked for King William III and Queen Mary II at Hampton Court. They may have been made by John Pelletier, a craftsman of French extraction. They support modern lustres copied from originals *c*.1775. The chandelier was recently bought for Duff House from Portsoy, and is English *c*.1820. The table on the west wall, with gilded entwined dolphins rising from a pedestal set with mirror glass is English, in 'Brighton Pavilion taste', *c*.1815–20, and comes from Dunimarle. The desk ('bureau plat') with kingwood veneer and ormolu mounts is stamped twice by Jacques Dubois (1694–1763, maître 1742), and the commode in kingwood, cedar and tulip wood with marble top is signed by Jean-Baptiste Hédouin (maître 1738, †1783). The ormolu clock with the Three Fates surmounted by an eagle is French, *c*.1810 or a little earlier. An ebonised and brass-inlaid cabinet displays a selection of Sèvres porcelain. All of these French works of art come from Dunimarle.

Crossing to the door to the right of the fireplace, we enter what is now a suite consisting of the **OUTER LIBRARY, STUDY**, and **INNER LIBRARY**, functions which none of these rooms originally performed. The Library was originally on the third floor on the west, and stretched along the entire west front, but this room is now reserved for educational use. We do know that James, 2nd Earl of Fife (1729–1809) was a bibliophile, with an extensive collection of books filled with portrait engravings, as well as a cabinet containing a large collection of Roman and British coins and medals. We also know he collected portraits of British Kings and Queens (which he displayed in the *Great*

Drawing Room). His elder brother, Louis, who died young and did not succeed, disagreed fundamentally with his father, who had joined the Duke of Cumberland in 1745 and made free offer of his services to Government in any way that might be desired. Louis had to be physically restrained from joining the Stewart cause. For this reason, it has been thought appropriate to hang the *Outer Library* with portraits principally of the Kings of Scotland, but the *Inner Library* with portraits of the exiled monarchs and Pretenders. The walls are furnished with handsome Chippendale-style oak bookcases, *c.*1762, originally from Monkton Hall House, Edinburgh, but filled with books principally from Dunimarle. The desk ('bureau plat') in the *Outer Library* is French, *c.*1750, and unsigned but so closely similar to that in the *Great* or *South Drawing Room* that it may also be by Dubois.

The STUDY, formerly a closet, has been used to house light-sensitive material, with the shutters closed and lit only by artificial light. It contains topographical and architectural drawings and water-colours associated with Duff House, its policies, and contents, and similar material from Dunimarle. Some items are facsimiles, where the originals cannot be shown.

In the INNER LIBRARY, the rich mahogany desk-chair, carved with rhyton-shaped arms consisting of fruit-filled cornucopia terminating in rams' masks, has the seat rail resting on lions of St Mark. From the Dunimarle Collection, it belonged to Napoleon's stepson, Eùgene de Beauharnais, Prince de Venise and Viceroy of Italy, 1805–14. The mahogany three-drawer desk, with turned legs and unusual voluted brackets, comes from Panmure House, Carnoustie, and belonged to James, Marquess Dalhousie KT (1812–60). The double sliding mahogany fire-screen in red morine is English or Scottish, *c.*1815. The pair of bergère arm-chairs, probably by Gillows of Lancaster, were supplied to Thomas Langford-Brooke of Mere Hall, Knutsford, Cheshire.

Eùgene de Beauharnais's chair

Over the chimneypiece hangs a rare and fascinating oil by William Delacour (fl. 1747–67), on loan from a descendant of the sitter. On the reverse is a hand-written label: *Sir Stuart Threipland Bart. dressed in the Belted plaid. An incident in his wanderings after the fatal Battle of Culloden – a Guardian Angel presents him with his shield. On the right the Government Troops, on the left the Highlanders. Painted by Delacour an Artist much patronised by the Jacobites.* To flank the picture are portraits of Flora MacDonald and Prince Charles Edward Stewart, while on the west wall hang portraits of James III (the 'Old Pretender') and his wife, Clementina Sobieska. Providing suitable tension at the tour's end is the portrait, from the studio of Sir Joshua Reynolds, of *The Duke of Cumberland*, adversary of the Bonnie Prince and victor at Culloden in 1746.

Detail from *Sir Stuart Threipland* by William Delacour

The History of Duff House

IAN GOW

The foundation stone of Duff House was laid on the 11th of June 1735. It is the grandest classical country house to be built on a fresh site in the early eighteenth century in Scotland; it is its architect, William Adam's masterpiece and one of the most important buildings in the North.

⤳ The Patron ⤳

The house was commissioned by William Duff (1697–1763), Lord Braco. The Duffs are an ancient Scottish family but the creation of their extensive network of estates had been recent and owed more to entrepreneurial flair than to traditional patterns of land holding. In 1734 he had decided not to stand again for parliament representing the County of Banff, 'and being resolved to settle at home; and his family pretty numerous, and yearly growing, he also resolved for his Amusement and better Accommodation' to improve his principal 'Mansion-House, near to the town of Banff'. This great project was to engage all his business skills and, where possible, each of his estates would contribute. Thus the timber was expected to come from his holdings in the Forest of Mar with the logs being floated down the Dee to Aberdeen and then shipped North. In

1723 he had built an austere but handsome new house to the designs of James Gibbs on his estate at Balveny and this perhaps gave him the confidence to act as his own 'undertaker' in the building of Duff.

Although his first intention was merely to improve the existing family property in the town and he had gone so far as to gather materials, engage the architect and appoint a supervising mason, there was a sudden change of heart, and a new site detached from the town was selected. Lord Braco was later to claim that it was the visit of 'ane honourable person of great Judgement and taste in Architecture' who advised him 'that a certain place Somewhat more distant from the Burrough of Banff, and building a new house there would be preferable to the proposed design of repairing or adding to the old house'. The grandeur of Duff, however, may also be explained by a temporary state of euphoria when the King recognised his financial and political success with the grant of an Irish peerage. At the outset there was perhaps an inherent tension in his desire to make 'a handsome or beautiful seat for his family' which had also to be managed 'in the most frugal and prudent Manner that such a thing could be done.'

William Duff, Lord Braco and his son, George and Jean Grant, Lady Braco and her son, Lewis by William Mosman, 1741

Opposite
Detail from a late 18th-century watercolour of Duff House

The Architect

It was Lord Braco's sense of doing things handsomely that must have led to the commissioning of William Adam (1689–1748) who was the leading architect at this time in Scotland. Adam's success arose from his mastery of the practical part of the mason's skills at the outset of his career alongside the development of his very real talent as a designer, particularly as a planner, through his many commissions. He also fully understood the need to reconcile his patrons' demands for ostentation and grandeur, characteristic of the Scots, with the actual informality of daily life in the country and their desire for comfort. Like Lord Braco, Adam had very considerable entrepreneurial flair and his activities extended beyond building and architecture to a proto-industrialisation that made him essential to patrons wishing to realise their ambitions in remote corners of Scotland with erratic funding. Adam had many important works and patrons to his credit, including the Earl of Hopetoun and the Duke of Hamilton, but Lord Braco was an important fish to have caught with his extensive resources and blatant ambition to put the family architecturally on the map of Scotland.

Marble bust of William Adam by unknown artist

The Design

Although keen to control costs, Lord Braco was an indulgent patron who left his chosen architect with a relatively free hand with the design. For Adam, who usually had to struggle to make intractable old tower houses fashionable and symmetrical, the request to design 'a magnificent family seat' for a wealthy peer on a fresh site, was the opportunity of a lifetime. Unfortunately no drawings have survived to document the evolution of the design. The final scheme, with its unrealised quadrant wings, is known only from the engraved version which Adam prepared for inclusion in his Vitruvius Scoticus. Although this must show the intention before 1740, when the turrets were finished differently, the dedication of the title plate to the 'Earl of Fife' proves that this plate must have been retouched after 1759, when the Earldom was granted to Lord Braco. The room usages, indicated on the plan, may also have been altered. In 1989, Historic Scotland commissioned Simon Montgomery to make a model of Adam's design to show the effect the wings would have had and this is displayed at the house.

In a new house symmetry could be respected. The arrangement of the plan reflects traditional Scottish patterns. The lowest floor was for service rooms, with additional services in the wings; the first floor was for the family above which was the piano nobile comprising a 'following' of rooms of state, approached by the grand staircase on a processional route through the house. Further bedrooms for guests were on the attic floor above. The principal rooms were arranged on a central axis with the great stair to one side on a cross axis through the centre of the house.

Adam's genius as a planner, however, enabled him to think in three rather than just two dimensions. Although a great house in the 1730s seems to have required relatively few reception rooms, there had been considerable specialisation in the design of individual bedroom apartments and for Duff Adam conceived a particularly ingenious and luxurious plan for these apartments which occupied each corner of both the family and the state floor. Although he must have been influenced by continental, and particularly French planning innovations, he was also working in an established Scottish tradition stretching back to Sir William Bruce for his

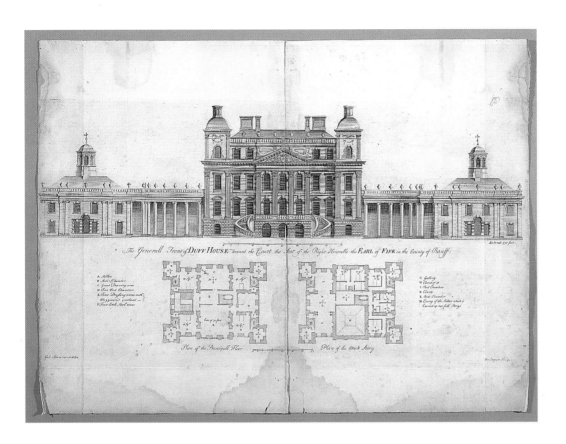

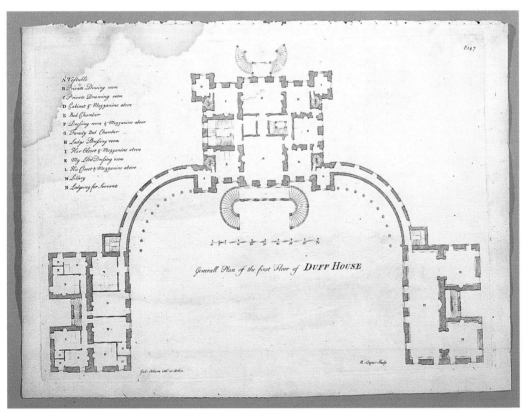

William Adam's published designs for Duff House from his *Vitruvius Scoticus*

own house at Kinross in 1679. Each apartment at Duff comprised a spacious square bedroom rising to a coved ceiling. Off this was a 'cabinet' or closet serving as a more intimate private space in the corner 'closet towers' which had proved a popular feature in Scottish architecture as a house like Marlfield shows. But by allowing for additional floor levels in the side elevations, as at Bruce's Kinross House, Adam was able to give each apartment servant's room in his 'mezzaninos'. In an additional luxury, each bedroom had a private 'stool room' in the space behind the service stair. Through his skill as a planner, Adam ensured that each of these interlocking spaces, and the circular service stairs themselves, were adequately lit by small windows in the side elevations. The placing of the service stair is particularly skilful, entering between the doors connecting each bedroom and closet to enable a servant to gain access to either room readily. Similarly, the grandest room of all, the 'Salon' or Great Dining Room in the centre of the principal front on the state floor rose up behind the pediment for thirty feet into the roofspace itself to form a perfect cube.

Although symmetry was paramount, Adam did not hesitate to break it for greater convenience and thus the main service stair, rising the full height of the house, was offset to make it as central as possible as befitted the primary route through the house. Duff House has therefore something of the same Baroque ingenuity as the architectural cabinets of that period with their intricate nests of secret drawers.

The external expression of this plan is also Baroque and the importance of the house is emphasised by the dominance of a single giant and flamboyant Corinthian order which marches round every facade, tightly binding the design under its oversailing cornice into a unity. It was exceptionally rare in Scottish architecture to have the resources to express an order in this costly way on every facade.

The Scots' fondness for piano nobiles at second floor level meant that their houses had a vertical thrust which Adam emphasised by giving his 'closet towers' Composite pilastered attic turrets rising to domes supporting octagonal chimneys into which the flues had been gathered. In the centre of the two principal fronts, the giant Corinthian pilasters support pediments with heraldic carving and statues, while at roof level the house bursts into a flourish of richly-carved vases and Vitruvian scrollwork. If these angle towers nod to Southern Palladian precedents, the effect is wholly Scottish and the vertical thrust allowed Duff to dominate the landscape for miles around and make the nearby town of Banff look like an appendage to the house. Adam's design is a fully integrated work of architecture with considerable expressive force.

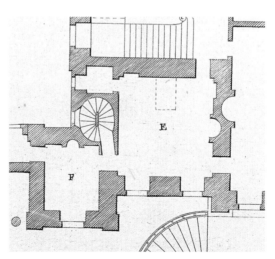

Detail of a bedroom apartment for Duff House from William Adam's *Vitruvius Scoticus*

◈ Building the House ◈

If Lord Braco was to fret at the expense, there can be no doubt that Adam's flamboyant design fully reflected his patron's ambitions for the future Duff dynasty and their power base in Banff. Because Lord Braco had the materials and foreman mason, John Burt, already on hand for additions to the old house, he was keen that 'the iron was struck while it was hot' and building proceeded rapidly. Adam attended the work once a year, when he stayed with the family as their guest, and at other times sent up the necessary designs and profiles, often at full size, for Lord Braco's masons. On account of illness, Adam did not appear in 1738 much to his patron's chagrin.

As the walls arose, and they got nearer the finer detail of the capitals, Burt grew concerned that they would demand the services of the best available masons in Scotland and that it might be difficult to lure them to Banffshire. Indeed, the ideal candidates, who were based near Jedburgh could hardly have been further away. Adam's solution, in discussion with Burt, was that Charles Burn, 'Stonecutter in Maxtoun' should carve the stone in Adam's own quarry near South Queensferry. It could then be conveniently shipped, with no excess weight, in the 'meal boats' which had to sail up to the North East for this cargo in any case. Unfortunately, as time was to show, Lord Braco somehow formed the idea that this wheeze would be cheaper than taking the mason himself to Banff whereas, to Adam, it was a device to maintain quality of execution. Certainly through Adam's direct supervision, the calibre of the ornaments was exceptional. Faced by an enquiry direct from his patron, after the first batch of ornaments arrived, as to what they had cost, Adam had brushed this aside and persuaded Lord Braco that it was more important to set them into place. They could worry about the bill later. During Adam's 'fourth and last visit' in 1739 the roof was put on and the 'shell' of this house was complete.

◈ The Law Courts ◈

Although disputes between architects and their patrons are not uncommon in architectural history, a peculiarity of that which burst over Duff was that the cause was not pursued until after this 'shell' had been completed to the highest possible specification and it was replete with every one of its phalanx of magnificent vases along the roofline. It was perhaps symptomatic of the souring of relationships that 'at the Beginning of Winter 1741' it was Lord Braco's lawyer who interviewed Adam and was presented with the accounts.

The final reckoning appeared to confirm Lord Braco's worst fears that he had been grossly overcharged, but, as the relationships further unravelled, all sorts of other grievances became magnified. It was Adam himself who was to raise a case for non-payment in 1743. The resulting hearings with the testaments of a very large number of witnesses including most of the craftsmen engaged on Duff, Adam's patrons and professional rivals make the Braco case the prime source of information about the Scottish building trades. The parties were well matched for a long and costly procedure. Lord Braco was not unaccustomed to bringing actions in the courts himself while Adam's business depended on taking risks by extending credit against future reward. Confusion was rife because there had been no proper contracts in the rush to build and Lord Braco must have suspected that he was caught up in the complex web of Adam's interconnected business empire. Even Lord Braco's own master mason had been Adam's appointee. Far from being cheaper to have had the ornaments cut at South Queensferry, Lord Braco's accountant considered that he had been over-charged by £5,000 and thus from 'one customer' Adam had therefore been ripping-off £1,000 each year or as much as the salaries of the highest officers in the land.

Lord Braco cruelly exposed the social pretensions inherent in Adam's dual stance as both professional architect and commercial builder and fixer. In Lord Braco's view he was himself the 'undertaker' of his own house because the men were paid directly through his employee, the master-mason, John Burt. Adam had been remunerated on each of his journeys North and thus Lord Braco was far from pleased with Adam's entry against the supply of plans including those for the additions to the old house. As architect, at the outset, Adam had airily written to his patron suggesting that he would 'cheerfully accept of what you shall think fit to give' while in his role as a builder, Adam charged by the measure, including his profit by the foot.

Although Adam was able to prove that this duality of role between architect and builder was the norm, and even the lack of contract was not unusual, Lord Braco, in his fury, was adept at dragging out the case beyond the obvious need for arbitration and third party measurement. Thus he made difficulties about permitting inspection pits so that the excavation foundations could be measured on the grounds that the fabric might be endangered and went so far as to detach one of the composite capitals so that it could be sent to London for inspection by the 'Earl of Carlisle, Lord Burlington, William Kent, John James of Greenwich Architect, Hawksmore and Gibbs'.

If Lord Braco derived satisfaction from the knowledge that this must all have been very damaging to Adam's other business ventures, it must have assuaged his vanity not a little to know that in terms of the costliness of his architectural ornaments he had eclipsed even Lord Hopetoun when Adam's carver testified that 'the Capitals and Vases for Lord Braco's House, cost the Deponent more Time and Trouble than any he had ever done of the same kind; being of a much larger Size, and more enriched'. The case cast a shadow over Adam's final years and he died on 24th June 1748.

⌁ *Fitting Out the Shell* ⌁

In popular mythology, Lord Braco remained so angry about Adam that Duff remained an abandoned shell for the rest of his life but he must have had more pressing reasons from being deflected from the task during the disruption of the 1745 Rebellion. His eldest son had had to be forcibly restrained from following Bonnie Prince Charlie and was otherwise unsatisfactory up to his death in 1753.

His second son, James, was to form more promising material to carry on a dynasty. In his childhood he went 'with his next brother, Alexander, to a country fair, each with a shilling in his pocket. Sandie's was soon spent, but James brought back the coin, saying 'he had seen naething he liked better nor the shilling'. A vivid picture of his character and original line of thought emerges from his letters which were edited by Alistair and Henrietta Tayler in *Lord Fife and his Factor 1729–1809*, 1925.

When work resumed at Duff in 1754 the news soon spread through the building trades, and Lord Braco received a number of petitions from tradesmen anxious to be considered for such an important task by such a wealthy patron. Their ranks included Francis Brodie the furniture-maker and Robert Dawson the plasterer but the job of fitting out the interior was entrusted to 'Thomas Dott, wright and cabinetmaker of Edinburgh'. This time there was to be no supervising external architect and a new emphasis on contracts.

There was a great deal to do from the construction of a temporary kitchen in what had been intended as the basement nursery below the family apartment, until such time as the wings were begun, alongside such essential tasks as installing glass in the window sashes. Work was concentrated on the basement and family rooms on the first floor. The piano nobile was left for a later campaign but the attic rooms on the third floor were fitted out in part because, without the wings, the house was short of bedrooms.

Although at least one of the attic rooms was panelled, fashionable taste had moved away from this method of finishing rooms as well as from the ornamental stucco latterly favoured by William Adam. The new Neo-Classical taste favoured understatement with plain wooden surbases and painted plain stucco or wallpaper above. Dott's work with its applied geometric fretwork is certainly provincial but, from the family papers, it is clear that a new personality is at work at Duff because Lord Braco's son James, known as the Master of Braco, was very much in evidence. Succeeding his father as Member of Parliament for Banff, the Master's taste was to become increasingly metropolitan although his activities were dutifully reported to his father who had not relinquished overall control:

'I wish you come down for a day or two to divert you, we are busy just now in preparing windows for the glass. Dott is to look over the account carefully.'

In the most important rooms like the Dining Room and Drawing Rooms there is a curious mixture of Inigo Jones and the French 'gout Grec', a taste the Master was to share with Sir William Chambers and it may be that he had access to sophisticated London advice as Dott wrote to Lord Braco in 1759:

'As for the vestibule I canot draw a plan of it Rightly

yet as the Master of Bracos not yet condeshended what way it is to be finished. He had carried the Dimenshens of to London with him to get advice about it there and he forbade Me to do any thing to it till I got further orders ....'

Unfortunately, the Master's London advisors are not recorded. Surprisingly, perhaps, Adam's sons were to supply marble chimneys from the family marble works. By 1757 the upholsterer John Schaw was temporarily fitting out some rooms with curtains, chair covers and beds and in 1759, the Dining Room and Drawing Room were ready for the painter, John Bonnar.

The year 1759 was important because Lord Braco was raised in the peerage to the rank of Earl of Fife and his eldest son, now Lord MacDuff, married Lady Dorothea Sinclair, the only child of the 9th Earl of Caithness. Duff House seems to have been made over to the newly married couple as Richard Pocock wrote to his sister on 28th July 1760: 'it is now inhabited by Lord MacDuff, Ld. Fife's Eldest son who is married to the sole heiress of the Earl of Caithness'. They occupied the family apartment on the first floor while the Countess of Fife retained the principal bedchamber on the first floor.

Although his first love was probably Fife House in London, which he had purchased in 1764 and where parliamentary duties detained him, he continued to improve Duff House and its park until his death. An inventory of Duff taken in 1761 reveals his Francophile rococo tastes in a suite of gilt pier glasses and matching pier tables decorated with carved birds but these were to remain its grandest furnishings. James Mackay had supplied similar furnishings for the Earl's earlier London house. By contrast, Fife House was to be sumptuously fitted up directly from Paris. The Great Room was altered to receive a suite of Gobelins tapestries. The designer of the room was Robert Adam which shows that Lord Braco's son did not bear a grudge and was determined that his London house should have the services of the greatest designer of his day.

⤳ *The Unbuilt Wings* ⤳

Although Duff in the early 1760s was now more than habitable, the lack of its wings was a serious inconvenience. The raggled masonry on the South West and South East 'closet towers' demonstrates the seriousness of the intent to add them from the outset. In 1766, Lord Fife complained of being 'pinc'd for Room till the Pavillions is built'. In 1759 a new detached kitchen had been built on the East side of the house to reduce the risk of fire spreading from its hearths. In 1764 the Earl was in touch with John Woolfe, a now rather obscure Irish architect, about a design for wings. It may be, however, that the design was a bi-product of Woolfe and his partner, James Gandon's, project to publish engravings of representative country houses in their *Vitruvius Brittanicus* and thus drum up commissions for themselves. Certainly as late as 1769, Woolfe was still trying to extract Lord Fife's opinion of the plans which he had presented for the wings and to gain more detailed information as to what the specification might be as to room usage. There was apparently an ambitious idea to remove the entire attic

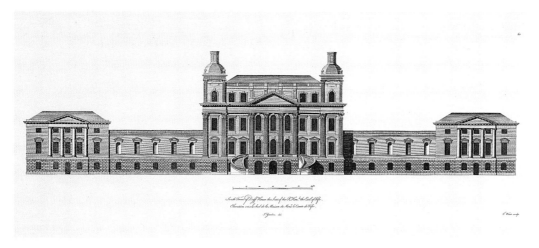

Design for wings at Duff House by James Gandon and John Wolfe from their continuation of *Vitruvius Britannicus*

story. Woolfe and Gandon's restrained Neo-Classical wings could not be more different from Adam's flamboyant colonnades and the Ionic order is their only common element. The internal arrangement of the plan does not appear to be particularly thoroughly worked out which leads one to question the degree of their patron's commitment to this paper pipe-dream. Their playing down of Adam's elaborate skyline gives credence to the idea that at some point in the evolution of their scheme the attic was to be eliminated. The inclusion, however of a top-lit picture gallery is the first sign of Lord Fife's mania for collecting that was to have a profound effect on the development of the house.

⤺ The Library ⤻

The fitting out of the third floor Library in 1774 was an admission, like the earlier Kitchen pavilion, that the wings with their generous library provision were no longer an immediate priority. The Earl had little incentive by now to proceed with more ambitious plans because his marriage had ended in separation and there had been no children, although he had had three illegitimate children during the 1750s by Margaret Adam of Keith.

It was the custom in Scotland to site country house libraries in a sequestered position on the attic floor away from the bustle of everyday life. The 'Gallery' shown in Adam's published plan, in the same position as the final library, may indicate a fail-safe against the late-arrival of the wings. Adam's most spectacular skied library is at Arniston House near Edinburgh which has resplendent glazed cases framed by Ionic columns and it featured in its own plate in Vitruvius Scoticus. In spite of the handsome scale of the library at Duff which stretched across the

entire West front and enjoyed fine views from windows on three sides, there was no attempt to create a room for show although Dott provided '20 Chinese doors' for the cases, a few of which still survive at its entrance door. Lord Fife's library was dedicated to serious purposes and particularly to his antiquarianism. Although books were by no means neglected it is clear that coins and medals were a particular enthusiasm. This interest perhaps led him on to portrait engravings as a key to unlocking his historical imagination.

In 1779, Charles Cordiner wrote to Thomas Pennant:

'since you were in this corner, a very large and elegant apartment is opened for a library; a well-proportioned room, of betwixt sixty and seventy feet in length. It is already stored with thousands of choice volumes; amongst them are vast collections of portraits of eminent persons, which prove a suitable accompaniment to a cabinet containing an extensive collection of Roman and British coins, medals etc.

The library extending through the whole breadth of the building, commands from the windows of one end, a charming prospect of the ocean, sea-coast, town of Banff and new bridge of seven arches thrown over the Deveron; from the other a fine extensive view into the country and of the pleasure grounds along the banks of the river.'

Lord Fife was a fuss-pot about the care of his precious collections and wrote, for instance, in 1789: 'I forgot to desire you to open the windows of the Library and lay the large books of prints on a table open in order to give them air and likewise to open the presses and air the books'. One of these volumes of prints was recently discovered bearing Lord Fife's bookplate, with portrait engravings of the Medici,

Decorative title and cartouche from the Duff House Library Catalogue, 1784 (Aberdeen University Library Special Collections)

Opposite
Engraving of Duff House after Charles Cordiner, 1779

in mint condition in a handsome binding testifying to a bibliophile's discernment. Lord Fife's delight in his books is reflected in the enchanting manuscript Catalogue of Books, 1784 with its decorative cartouches surrounding the case letters and ornamental flourishes in watercolour.

Such was the scale of his collecting that a 'pamphlet' library had soon to be fitted up in a nearby room but it was the expansion of the picture collection that obliged him to fit up the second floor in the late 1780s.

∽ The Picture Collection ∽

Lord Fife's personal pride in his picture collection is reflected in the Catalogue he himself wrote and had printed in 1807 with a dedication to Sir Benjamin West, President of the Royal Academy. Unusually, perhaps, Lord Fife's interest focused on portraits and, like his antiquarianism, may have grown out of an interest in the origins of the Duff family:

'Being possessed of several good portraits which belonged to my family, I began many years since to make additions to them. I have lately had an opportunity of increasing my Collection, so that I believe, there are few more numerous.'

The seriousness of his purpose and his desire to rescue early likenesses from oblivion is also made clear in the Preface to his Catalogue in a way that anticipated the later idea of a National Portrait Gallery:

'It is surprising how often curious old portraits are found in places where nobody almost would ever think of looking for them. They are often thrown out of the houses for lumber, the name of the Artist and Person represented being unknown, or are sold to pay debts or to make way for the modern fashion of papering rooms. I know many houses, where very fine Portraits are put up to garrets, and neglected, while their places are supplied with an eightpenny paper.'

The range of his collection is remarkable and reflects his original line of thought. While many strands are conventional like the sub-groups of kings and queens, artists' portraits and beauties or royal mistresses, the emphasis on early, and thus often obscure, likenesses is unusual. Although there was a clear attempt to segregate groups in display so that the Duff family pictures were hung together in the public rooms used by the family themselves,

and the Great Drawing Room was the exclusive province of British Kings and Queens, the ever expanding collection resulted in some strange juxtapositions to an extent where it is interesting, if fanciful, to speculate on what the portraits might have had to say to one another as 'Sir John and Lady Hart Lord Mayor of London 1589 by Cornelius Jansen' and 'Nell Gwynn Three Quarters Mother to the Duke of St Albans Van Dyke' found themselves in each other's company.

Lord Fife pioneered the study of historic costume to help date new accessions. His interest, as his notes on the pictures show, was more firmly rooted in the biographies of the sitters than their artists. His passion for other people's ancestors must have been well known as many pictures came as presents. The disruption following the French Revolution after 1789 allowed Lord Fife to intersperse his motley band with a dash of French royals, yet more royal mistresses and leading politicians. He had a field day at Sir Joshua Reynolds's studio sale.

Lord Fife had less interest in conventional old masters although the Drawing Rooms at Fife House in London had the inevitable Raphael, Titian and a Rubens. Portraits predominated at Duff and his other country houses including Innes, Dalgaty and Rothiemay. His major act of patronage of a living artist was perhaps typically a series of matter-of-fact views of his seats, including Duff by the topographical artist, William Tomkins. The Scottish views hung in their own room at Fife House while Tomkins views of Fife House, one of which included *A Favourite Dog (called Dick)* hung in the Parlour at Duff.

The fitting out of the piano nobile at Duff in the late 1780s was therefore as much to display the cream of this very large collection as to fulfil any very serious practical needs and it is thus particularly appropriate in the 1990s that these rooms should have found a new use as an art gallery.

As intended by Adam the largest room in the centre of the entrance front behind the pediment would have been the Great Dining Room or Salon, leading to a Great Drawing Room off which would lie the State Bedroom with its dressing room, closet and backstairs. Adam's contemporary section of the Salon at Culter, near Aberdeen for Patrick Duff of Premnay, a cousin of the First Earl of Fife gives some idea of what Adam might have intended with stucco decorations and decorative painting.

By the 1780s, however, state apartments were no longer a pre-requisite of country house plans even for prominent peers.

Lord Fife, in directing the new works, stressed an emphasis on simplicity 'I wish to have a plan and Estimate for the two large rooms at Duff House I intend to make the present cube just 25 feet in height, so I think when the Stair and those two rooms are done there I shall do little more let the next do the rest' and in 1790 he wrote 'I intend to paper the two large rooms and hang pictures over them'. This simplicity, however, was not solely the product of frugality because to a man of Lord Fife's fashionable taste this cult of understatement was shared by his most sophisticated contemporaries in the 1790s and the resulting rooms, with their composition chimneypieces, sent up from London, were austerely elegant.

Two inventories of 1795 and 1809 reveal that there was no very serious attempt to use the rooms as anything other than as picture galleries and there was a noticeable lack of expenditure on other furnishings.

In 1793 Lord Fife turned his attention to building a Mausoleum in the Park and, reflecting his interest in antiquarianism, it was in a Gothic style but it was not to be until 1809 that he was laid to rest within its walls after a remarkable fifty years of stewardship of Duff House.

⤳ *The Fourth Earl* ⤳

With no legitimate heir, the 2nd Earl had taken a great interest in the eldest son of his brother Alexander and saw that he was carefully groomed for his future responsibilities. Alexander, however, was to outlive his brother and thus became the 3rd Earl of Fife. He seems to have done very little at Duff beyond repapering the Dining Room with flock and hanging the Drawing Room with a glazed paper during the winter of 1809–10, immediately after his accession. At the same time some of the curtains were remade or replaced by fashionable French-style draw curtains instead of the eighteenth century festoon draw-up curtains.

The 4th Earl succeeded his father in 1811. His remarkable career was the subject of a ponderous but deeply felt biographical tribute in James Imlach's History of Banff, 1868, which testifies to the very great affection in which he was held by the people of Banff.

After an education supervised by his uncle, and the run of the libraries at both Duff and Fife House, a military career was selected and he was thus to serve on the continent at the outset of the Napoleonic wars. After his return, he married Mary Caroline Manners in 1799, who was the daughter of the Countess of Dysart. Sadly, his wife died in 1805 and they had had no children. 'Overwhelmed by grief' he sought solace in foreign travel and was soon, and perhaps inevitably, caught up in the Peninsular Wars and he headed for Spain to join he patriots. He was wounded at Talavera, befriended by Wellesley and wounded again in the heroic defence of the Fort of Matagora. After his father's death in 1811 he was obliged to return home but not before he had been awarded the rank of General by the Cortes and made a grandee of Spain.

He returned a war hero and was 'received with eclat at the Court of the Prince-Regent, who regarded him with special favour, and soon conferred on him the office of Lord of the Bedchamber'.

To someone of such cosmopolitan exposure, Duff House, which was more art gallery than country house must have seemed both old-fashioned and austere and the 4th Earl was soon embarked on a campaign of redecoration. Indeed, his Spanish years had resulted in the acquisition of a collection of Spanish pictures, many of them being gifts, which required suitable display in an already over-pictured house. The Spanish pictures added a very unusual and special character and one, *The Infant Saviour with the Crown of Thorns* was a particular favourite with visitors. They also diluted the predominantly portrait character of the house.

Imlach wrote of his life at Duff:

'At various periods since his return from Spain, when he could withdraw himself from Court, and his personal attendance on the Sovereign, we find him at home, at his princely seat, Duff House, doing the honours of his house and of his high position in the most liberal hospitality. His receptions were of the most recherché character, and given with a splendour and taste seldom witnessed in the far north, and at his table you met the highest personages in the land. On these

festive occasions, the extensive and magnificent range of apartments were thrown open and filled with hundreds of the great, the gay and the happy for days in succession.

At this time his Lordship's household was under the direction of a personage of high taste and skill in decorative and entertaining art – a second Gunter – so these festive scenes were not inaptly designated "The Arabian Nights' Entertainments". On occasions when his Lordship's visitors were confined to the family circle, as he generally had a few select spirits in his coterie, his menage and daily routine were perfect, and would have satisfied the most exquisite gourmand. His French cuisinier was highly skilled in the art, and produced the most perfect displays; while from his Lordship's most perfect knowledge of the qualities of all sorts of wines, the various kinds with which the tastes of his guests were plied became instructive and no doubt happily exhilirating.'

The architect James Gillespie (who subsequently added Graham to his own surname in honour of his wife) seems to have been responsible for advising on these home improvements and certainly no Scottish architect had greater interest in either interiors or theatrical decorative effects. The principal surviving feature of this 'splendour and taste' are the painted decorations executed by the Edinburgh painter, John Jackson. Dating from 1814 they are amongst the earliest examples of a revival of a taste for ornamental painting in Scotland and Jackson owed his opportunity to his patron's familiarity with the extravagant decorations of the Prince Regent's many expensive residences. In 1818 Jackson employed the young David Roberts, at Craigcrook Castle, for Francis Jeffrey and at the Duke of Lauderdale's house at Dunbar and was remembered by Roberts as 'a well known decorative painter, and a sincere lover and patron of art'.

Rich new furniture and drapery followed and is poignantly described in the 'Catalogue of elegant and costly furniture Scarce and Rare Paintings, Prints and other valuable effects, To be sold by auction by Warrant of the Sheriff of Banffshire, October 1824'. Lord Fife was certainly extravagant but his difficulties arose because 'His uncle's extraordinary testament had curtailed his expectancies, which obliged him to have recourse to law proceedings, which involved him in heavy losses.' The problem was that the 2nd Earl had both entailed as much of the estate as possible in order to ensure the continuance of his careful stewardship and the survival of his 'personal collections of pictures, plate, coins etc' while leaving as much as he possibly could to benefit his elder illegitimate son, to whom he had always been close, for the rest of his life.

Like the Arabian Nights' Fantasy that it had been the high life at Duff suddenly faded away and the depth of the subsequent financial stringency can be glimpsed in the various attempts to reduce the taxable burden on the house:

'Now nothing can be better known to your Honours than that the whole of the Furniture of Duff House belonging to Lord Fife was sold off before the commencement of the period to which the present Appeal applies And it is a fact capable of being easily established that any articles of furniture now within Duff House are parts of what was sold but which still remain in the house the property of others until they can be conveniently removed by the purchasers or belong in property to the Trustees of the late Earl of Fife.'

The solution had therefore been savage retrenchment but it does look as though, from the priced catalogue, that the neighbours had rallied around and bought at least some of the furniture whose description is certainly recherché as in the 'superb gilt conversation chair with Green cover' or the 'Four Small, and One Arm curious Ivory Chairs, with Fine Crimson velvet seats'.

After such a brilliant start to his life at Duff it is sad to think of the 4th Earl, who spent much of his time at Duff after 1833, living in reduced circumstances but the gainers were the people of Banff who 'owed him a debt of gratitude for the increased measure of health they enjoyed in the free admission to his beautiful park and gardens'. He died at Duff in February 1857.

❧ The Fifth Earl ❧

The 4th Earl, like the second, was also succeeded by his nephew. Duff's royal connections continued because the 5th Earl had married in 1846 Lady Agnes Hay, daughter of the Earl of Errol and Lady Elizabeth Fitzclarence, whose father was William IV. Of great significance for the future was Queen Victoria's acquisition of the lease of Balmoral which made the Queen the Fifes' neighbour at Mar Lodge.

Opposite
Detail of the Dining Room showing the portrait of The 2nd Earl of Fife after Francis Cotes and candelabra which belonged to the 4th Earl

The Duff they inherited must have been tinged by a sense of faded grandeur and, possibly with limited resources, they set out to bring it up to date with the Countess directing the interior decorations. The Countess had a particular interest in interior decoration and practised her hand in her earlier home at Skene House as well as Corriemulzie Cottage on the Mar estate. The character of her efforts has been recorded in a series of photographs of the principal rooms which suggest that this task was entrusted to an as yet unidentified North East firm whose stamp can also be identified in old photographs of Cullen and Castle Fraser – they were certainly not a sophisticated London firm but must have had sufficient probity to attract the favour of the local aristocracy. The North Drawing room photographs show a suite of high Victorian furniture diluting the effect of the 2nd Earl's massed ranks of portraits. The Countess was to die in 1869 at the early age of fifty as the result of a fall from her carriage.

The most significant change came in 1870, following the Countess's death, when David Bryce, Junior, was commissioned to add a new Kitchen and Bedroom wing. Built on the site of the 1759 detached Kitchen, it perhaps owed a little to Woolfe and Gandon, but, and characteristic of the Bryces' work was not only understated but took its cue from the original building with perfect tact. The plan reveals that in addition to more extensive Kitchen accommodation, the first floor contained a top-lit Billiard Room but was otherwise partitioned into nests of bedrooms which until then were in short supply. Bryce managed to link old and new ingeniously by partitioning the old family bedchamber, so that, with minimal disturbance, there was considerable gain in practicality. These modest changes enabled the house to cope with the large house parties of the late nineteenth century.

∽ *The First Duke* ∽

The 5th Earl died in 1879 and was succeeded by his eldest son Alexander who in 1889 married Princess Louise, the eldest daughter of the Prince of Wales, later Edward VII and he was made Duke of Fife. Princess Louise subsequently became Princess Royal.

The Prince of Wales had stayed at Duff House from 13–17 November 1883, arriving by a special train. The townspeople demonstrated their loyalty through extravagant temporary decorations in their houses and their shops. The Ball held annually at Duff on the Earl's birthday was rescheduled to take place during the Prince's stay. The Prince's visit was marked in the traditional way by the planting of a commemorative tree and he was presented with a handsome photograph album depicting local scenery as a souvenir.

But Duff could hardly have been considered a satisfactory residence for the future Princess Royal and it was Mar Lodge that was to be rebuilt, after a fire in 1895, as a more suitable residence. Duff House was to become a casualty of the financial difficulties that marked many great estates in the late nineteenth century and was offered by The Duke and Duchess of Fife to the towns of Banff and Macduff in 1906. Duff thus became one of the earliest Country Houses to have to find a new non-domestic role. The subsequent history of the Duke and Duchess of Fife was marked by tragedy. The Duke died at Aswan as a result of the exposure he suffered when

Left Arch erected to welcome the Prince of Wales to Banff

Right House party with the Prince of Wales on the steps of Duff House

42

Left The Bryce wing at
Duff House

Right Duff House forlorn
after the Second World War

the S.S. Delhi was shipwrecked on their way to
Egypt. He was buried at Mar Lodge. The Duchess
lived in retirement until 1931. The present Duke of
Fife is descended from their younger daughter, who
married the Earl of Southesk.

∽ Duff in the Twentieth Century ∽

Duff House found a new future, at first as an hotel.
The advertising brochure played up the House's
royal connections and the sporting activities previously reserved for the family and their guests. The
management were at pains to stress this continuity:
'no effort has been spared to carry out a scheme of
furnishings to be in keeping with the surrounding
beauties'. The hotel company transformed the
rooms with schemes of imitation panelling comprising mouldings, stuck over paper lining, which
had the effect of carefully preserving Jackson's
painted decorations. The hotel's pretensions, however, may have over-reached the potential market
because by 1913 it had become a sanatorium. Duff
House thus became a 'private hospital for the inves-
tigation and treatment of disorders of nutrition'.
The sanatorium's brochure shows that it was equp-
pied with the very latest technology. By 1923, however, this new venture had proved so successful that
it outgrew the available accomodation and sought
new premises at Ruthin Castle in Wales. From
1923–8, Duff was once again run as an hotel but its
brochure perhaps reveals a less ambitious assess-
ment of the potential market than its predecessor.

Duff House was requisitioned at the start of the
Second World War and housed German prisoners
of war. The Bryce wing was seriously damaged by a
stray Luftwaffe bomb. Norwegian and Polish troops
were subsequently quartered at Duff and several
rooms still bear traces of their grafitti and stencilled
notices.

After the war the future of Duff House looked
extremely bleak and contemporary photographs
record its ravaged state. It owed its survival to its
sheer architectural quality. A Minute in the files of
the Ministry of Works dated 1952 described how:
*'Every effort has been made to put the building to use
but in vain. It seems that if the Ministry do not take
over this fine example of architecture in the grand
manner it will be demolished.'*

Fortunately, the Ministry did take Duff in hand
and, little by little, the air of dereliction departed and
the House's very considerable architectural merit re-
asserted itself. Bomb damaged masonry was carefully repaired by the craftsmen of the Ancient
Monuments Branch and the roof was put in sound
order. With a limited budget, until a new use could
be found for the house, the interior began to be
restored suficiently to permit some public access as
the previous guidebook of 1985 by Professor A.
A.Tait reveals. During this time a programme of
research was undertaken into the surviving family
papers. A complete transcript of all the references to
the building and decoration of the House was prepared to guide the restoration. This guidebook has
drawn freely on this transcript.

None of this would have been possible, however,
had the superlative quality of Adam's carved ornaments, the cause of so much strife in the 1740s, not
continued to shine through during the lowest ebb in
the House's fortunes two hundred years later.

The Architecture and Decoration of Duff House

IAN GOW

∽ The South Front ∽

The entire facade is embraced by the giant Corinthian order pilasters with their richly carved capitals supporting the pediment in the centre. The arcaded windows below the pediment light the Saloon which was to rise 30 feet up into the roofspace on the piano nobile while those below light the entrance hall. The corner 'closet towers' bear composite pilasters and their domed turrets support convex fluted octagonal chimneys into which their flues are gathered.

The architectural ornaments were all carved in Adam's quarry at South Queensferry and shipped North complete. Each element is accounted for individually in Adam's bills. The capitals, which are composed of several stones, cost 20 guineas each. The deeply undercut heraldic tympanum of the pediment was also cut at Queensferry, where its stones must have been temporarily clamped together, at a cost of 150 guineas. High above the balustrades support a phalanx of richly carved vases whose different patterns are detailed in the bills. They must owe something to the plates of vases in Gibb's Book of Architecture and are a staggering 5 foot high and also cost 20 guineas each.

There are signs of difficulties in incorporating the ready-made capitals into pre-established wallplanes as well as retrenchment in unfinished details. Although the swags of drapery high up on the turrets have been carved, what were intended to be palm-fronds above them, like the keystones above the entrance hall windows, remain uncut. A curious spur to the left of the second capital from the west is a further sign, perhaps, that the scaffolding was struck during the legal dispute and the details were never finished. Such is the complexity of the architecture, however, that a few details, although finished, have an unresolved effect like the belt at second floor level which simply stops when it meets the flutes of the giant pilasters. This belt was to be carried through onto the wings.

The lead statues on the pediment may be another economy because they were transferred from 'the bowling green' of the town house and so may have begun their life as garden ornaments. They certainly seem, in their very quality, to have been intended to be seen at closer quarters and are perhaps too small in scale. By reducing the height of his Saloon, the 2nd Earl gained additional attic rooms above it. These were latterly lit by triangular windows on either side of the pediment but have now been filled in with stone.

∽ The East Front ∽

The oblique view of the closet towers reveals the complexity of the internal planning at Duff through Adam's use of his 'mezzaninos'. It becomes obvious that only the lower zones of the large windows in the South fronts of the towers light the low rooms behind and each closet has a servant's room above. Adam's skill as a planner allowed him to light each of these spaces effectively. On the side facade the position of the central staircase is obvious through the landing-height placement of its great arched windows. The small windows on both sides of the projecting stair light the corner spiral staircases in the angles and the inner stool rooms with mezzanine storage rooms above them respectively. Neither swags nor palm-fronds are carved on this or any of the other fronts. The rough masonry to the South shows where the wings would have projected from the South West closet tower. Lord Braco, at one stage baulked at the cost of the pilasters continuing on the side facades but this potential economy as so often at Duff was abandoned. The entire third floor on this facade was given over to the library. The basement of the South West Tower and the room adjoining were fireproofed muniment rooms, an important specialised room usage in Scotland and a necessary requirement for the litigious Lord Braco.

Opposite
The centrepiece of the South Front

The side-door in the basement gives access to a corridor through the house.

∽ *The North Front* ∽

It is quite exceptional in Scottish architecture to have two such grand show fronts on a single house and there is no diminution in grandeur. The tympanum is no less richly carved than that on the South front but here Lord Braco's arms are quartered with those of his wife, Jean Grant of Grant, Lady Braco. In 1759 it was decided to dispense with the perron designed by Adam on this front and the central door was built up to form a window. The later eighteenth-century fitting up of the Drawing Room on the second or State floor is reflected in its comparatively slender, and almost metallic, sashes which contrast with Adam's heavier joinery. Windows above the Drawing Room light attic rooms because the former was lower than the Saloon on the South front. The three central windows in the basement lit the Parlour, which was the only room on the ground floor in daily use by the family, but it was probably only used when there were no guests.

∽ *The West Front* ∽

Repeats the East Front, except that the Stair is balanced by a pair of bedrooms, the lower of which was the family bedroom with both Lord and Lady Fife having a complete adjacent apartment with its mezzanines for their personal use. The room behind the South East Turret on the ground floor was intended by Adam as the Nursery and a similar arrangement survives at his House of Dun. Bryce's wing has left a scar, as also have the glazed balconies erected during Duff's spell as a hospital, although the stonework has been most carefully repaired by the Ancient Monuments craftsmen. The South East corner also shows traces of bomb damage.

The North Front

∽ The Vestibule ∽

The Vestibule was intended as the principal entrance to the house after the building of the perron in 1760, although in ordinary usage the door below the perron would have been used by the staff and family. It was the custom in the early eighteenth century for halls to be simply decorated and treated almost as outdoor spaces. The 2nd Earl, as Lord MacDuff, is known to have taken advice in London on the fitting out of this room. The walls would have been plain-painted over the flush wooden surbase and the chimneypiece with its carved trusses has also been treated simply, but there is a degree of sober enrichment in the pedimented doorcases with their pulvinated friezes decorated with leaves. The great central arched door echoes that of the main entrance and is decorated with Vitruvian scrolls and carved rinceau. Its glazed upper section lights the lobby leading to the dining room behind.

Somewhat at odds with this plainness below is the rather riotous rococo ceiling, the only ornamented stuccowork in the entire house, with its deeply undercut rose for a central lamp. The design reflects the 2nd Earl's Francophile rococo taste with its exotic birds and naturalistic foliage and fruits. With its theme of vine leaves it is possible that the Vestibule, as the largest completed room in the house during the 1760s, might also be pressed into service as the dining room on festive occasions. The plasterwork was probably sub-contracted out by Dott to 'David Crooks ornamental Plaisterer' of whom nothing is known. His work is a mixture, like much of this period at Duff, of elegance of design, in the way, for instance that the birds tug at the garlands of flowers, alongside a certain naïvety, bordering on coarseness, noticeable in the almost naïve masks at the centre of each side but it is certainly technically accomplished in its depth of projection.

The Vestibule c.1870

47

This room also had a 'stucco' floor which was to be a source of trouble and later was replaced by cement.

In the 1761 Inventory this room, like most halls, was very simply furnished with twelve mahogany chairs with leather seats, a portrait of George II, who granted the family their peerage, and a large painting of dead game. The King's picture may have formed a unit with the chimneypiece. By 1795 the room was more fully furnished not only with more pictures spreading over the wall faces but with more tables and chairs. Its most exotic item was a 'macaw with a Glass frame', preserving in death, one of the house's liveliest and certainly the most colourful inhabitants: 'A Macaw from the West Indies lived in the house from 1756 to 1784'. There was even more furniture in 1809 including '2 stand of Colours – Banffshire Volunteers'. It may be that this attractive sunny room took on more of the character of a living room, being conveniently placed at the centre of the house.

The bands of bas-relief ornaments around the walls are by John Jackson of Edinburgh in 1814 and conform to a scheme which he first suggested for the Parlour:

'As the Parlour has been formerly painted I can make it very elegant again and would propose making it a Rose colour with white and gold Bas Relieve ornaments with painted ceiling which will have a very fine effect'.

Jackson carefully copied the rinceau from the large doorcases on the inside corners and there is a sense in which it has all been laid out freehand whereas later decorative painting would at least have been laid out with a stencil. Known from the early photographs, this decoration was discovered behind later imitation panelling and restored by the Stenhouse Conservation Centre in the late 1970s when the fictive panelling on the flat dado was also repainted.

This room is shown in no less than three early photographs of *c.*1870 recording Countess Agnes's decorations. The high-backed Charles II style chairs were standard components of early Victorian Scottish halls and were intended to give an antiquarian effect. The Hall character has been overlaid, however, by the rococo drawing-room components which take their cue from the glittering overmantel glass which presumably was part of the 2nd Earl's original furnishings, although resited. Too narrow

in width, it has been judiciously stretched to fit by additional gilt ornaments at the sides. The design is similar to some of Thomas Johnson's plates in his *Collection of Designs,* 1758 .

The Louis XV style chairs may be from Fife House in London but their original line has been plumped up with Victorian deep-sprung upholstery. Of the two photographs of the West wall, the more informal shot may show the normal state of the house under wraps when the family was away. The chairs are covered with chintz loose covers and the glass globes from the chandelier in store. The second photograph, probably taken at the same time, shows, the photographer re-arranging the furniture to highlight the bust of Countess Agnes by Brodie flanked by her photographs, framed in deep black borders. The bust was elaborately decorated on the day of her funeral at Duff. In the late-nineteenth century the Duke and Duchess of Fife used this room as their Dining Room. It must have been the hotel company who redecorated the Vestibule in imitation of dark panelling with applied mouldings over paper (which had reached a sorry state by the 1950s) and laid the parquet floor.

✎ *The Dining Room* ✎

Traditionally, Dining Rooms were the most splendidly decorated rooms in the Scottish country house through being the largest and most richly ornamented. That at Duff is no exception and is given importance through the application of an Ionic order giving a very architectural effect. The correctness of the interior architecture, in contrast to the naïvety elsewhere at Duff in the 1750s, is the result of the doorcase leading from the Vestibule being copied from the engraving drawing of the Chapel at Somerset House in London in Isaac Ware's Designs of Inigo Jones, 1731, and it is possible that many of the other details at Duff are quotations, or variations, on similar published sources. The 'dove colour'd' marble chimneypiece was supplied by John and James Adam from their Edinburgh marble works in April 1759 and came with 'best white Chimney Tiles'. The trusses at the sides may have been assembled upside down. The applied timber mouldings on the wall face give a very formal effect and were presumably always intended to be filled by the family portraits.

The Vestibule *c.*1870

In complete contrast with these walls is the very frivolous ceiling which is the most unusual feature of the room because it is made of papier mâché and was certainly in place by June 1761 when Dott charged for '4 pound white Lead for washing the paper Mashie Ceiling of the Dining Room of Duff House'. Manufacturers in London, like Bromwich, were trying to develop this material as a substitute for plasterwork but they soon exploited its individual characteristics. An account from Bromwich survives for the supply of mouldings to Lord MacDuff in 1762. The overall effect is much flatter than the plasterwork of the Vestibule but the lacework inside the corner ornaments is unique to the possibilities of papier mâché and would simply not be possible in plaster. The ceiling is composed of stock components, selected to fill the area of its bed, and the elements were simply pinned into place, being exceptionally light. The rather jaunty doileyesque border is somewhat at odds with the severe and proper Ionic pulvinated entablature.

Papier mâché would have had an immediate appeal for Lord Fife because he had a particular aversion to the 'dirt' stirred up by builders and so the cleanliness of installing this material would have endeared it to him. High up in the North East turret there is a second papier mâché ceiling in chinoiserie style with pagodas and Chinamen and these commercial components were perhaps aimed more at smaller boudoirs and dressing rooms than formal rooms like the Dining Room. Unfortunately this Chinoiserie ceiling cannot be on public view.

The rococo character of the ceiling was continued by dazzling gilt chinoiserie pier tables and glasses which are described in the 1761 Inventory: *'Two fine Marble Tables, on fine Gilt Standarts, wt. the figure of a large Gilt Bird on each Table and Two Large Looking Glasses in fine Carved Gilt Frames, with figures of three birds on top of each glass' and a 'fine Gilt Sconce, with three branches for Candles, a large Branch on the Top, with figures of two Birds'*

These pier tables and glasses with the other rococo glasses at Duff were all acquired by Partridges, the London art dealers, after the sale of the contents. It was unusual for dining rooms to be fitted out with so much mirror glass but this may reflect the constrained accommodation in the early years of Duff.

The room always contained family portraits and these became more distinguished through the years. The Countess was painted in full length by Reynolds, the Earl by Cotes and earlier members of the family by Ramsay and Mossman. Lord Fife's two illegitimate sons were subsequently included. The blocks over the doors supported 'Busts of the plaister of Paris, Coloured' and the curtains were always of red damask.

By the 1809 Inventory there was also a red morocco settee in addition to conventional Dining Room furniture and a 'Finger Organ and a Barell do. (6 Barrels)'. During the time of the 4th Earl, whose portrait in the dress of a Spanish General by Raeburn over the chimneypiece added to its splendour, the table decorations were very elaborate as surviving pieces of his plate show. One of the last changes to this room was in 1853 when Charles Cameron replaced the central panel on the West wall opposite the chinmney-piece with a mirror plate at the cost of £26. The Duke and Duchess of Fife used this room as a Library.

⤳ The Private Drawing Room ⤶

This room is labelled 'Private Drawing Room' on Adam's *Vitruvius Scoticus* plan but the plate may have been recut when its dedication was altered in, or after, 1759 when the Earldom was granted. By the mid-eighteenth century a Drawing Room (as against the old Withdrawing Room of a State Apartment) was deemed as an essential prerequisite and thus a complete bedroom apartment was sacrificed to this new function as the 1761 Inventory confirms. The very decorative finish carved by Dott was appropriate to a Drawing Room. There is an attempt at unity of effect through the repetition of the square fret on the overdoors and chimney surround. This fret, like the twisted swags on the chimneypiece are very much in an advanced French 'gout Grec' taste characteristic of early Neo-Classicism, even if the expression is provincial, and it may be that Lord MacDuff was either paying for sophisticated advice or feeding Dott with fancy engravings which he struggled to master.

The marble slips of the chimneypiece were supplied by John and James Adam in 'statuary marble' and are an early example in Scotland of the choice of this flawless white marble for a Drawing Room which later became the convention. The 1761 and 1795 Inventories reveal that this room too had a fine pier glass and table and chimneyglass: 'a marble side board wt. indented cards and Gilt carved stand' and 'a large ornamented Gilt framed mirror over the Chimny', 'Another Do Do between the windows'. From a later account, when the pier table had moved elsewhere in the house it is clear that the table had either a pietra dura or scagliola top 'its grey mottled marble top inlaid with playing cards, resting on one of Adam's gilt extravagances, representing a tree and a heron fishing beneath it, attract attention'.

The presence of a 'Settee Bed' in 1761 is perhaps a reflection of the shortage of bedrooms at the house when the Drawing Room would be pressed into service if there were a number of guests. There were yellow damask curtains in 1761 but they were green by 1795 and the walls were painted 'fine green' in 1795 with the woodwork 'dead white'. There were quantities of pretty china and '2 Black stucco heads over the doors'. In 1795 ten small early family pictures of the Duffs hung here but by the time of the picture Catalogue of 1807 these were reduced to only four early non-family portraits including Queen Elizabeth and the room had become 'The Red Damask Bed Chamber'.

The reduction of the portraits was possibly to make way for the 'Tapestry A fine Piece of Goblens Tapestry, from Coypel, the French Painter' around which the room was probably redecorated. In *Summer Excursions in the Neighbourhood of Banff*, 1843 this was described glowingly as:

'a large specimen of the celebrated Gobelin tapestry. The design was made by Coypell, a famous French painter. The execution of the figures and of the landscape and architecture is surprisingly beautiful, while the vividness and glow of the colours, particularly the various shades of red, are such as could hardly be imagined to be excelled'

This panel must have been connected with Lord Fife's improvements at his London house. Lord Fife had employed Willam Donn to alter his London house, re-christened Fife House, after its purchase in 1764. The rectangular Great Room, with a bow window at one end, already existed and was redesigned by Robert Adam in 1766 to take a suite of Gobelins tapestries woven in France under the direction of Jacques Neilson. This ensemble at Fife House was one of a group of similar tapestry rooms commissioned with especial enthusiasm by English patrons. These include the tapestry room at Croome Court in Worcestershire (now transferred to the Metropolitan Museum of Art in New York) and the set woven for Sir Laurance Dundas at Moor Park in Hertfordshire, which after its installation in two other houses belonging to the Marquess of Zetland, is now most appropriately on loan to Duff House.

The skill of their design arose because their principal decorative feature comprised small panels, conceived as fictive framed pictures, hung against a 'damask' ground. By judicious alterations and additions to the borders, sets could be woven to fit particular rooms. The splendour of Lord Fife's room was reflected in huge plate glasses, also manufactured in France. Lord Fife desired a further vast plate of glass over the chimneypiece but was dissuaded by Adam who felt that continuing the tapestry across the entire wall would have a grander effect. Lord Fife also desired white and green velvet curtains and upholstery until it was explained that the whole point of the damask ground, and he had selected crimson as the background colour, was that the curtains could be made up in matching damask and Lord Fife soon succumbed to ordering 'Crimson Genoa damask' to suit. Robert Adam designed an exceptionally rich ceiling for the Great Room. At one stage during the discussions the seat furniture was also to be covered in tapestry made up by Mayhew and Ince, the London upholsterers. The tapestry was brought in via Holland, possibly to evade customs duty, and the room was completed with a display of French porcelain. Although the Moor Park tapestries bear scenes depicting the 'Loves of the Gods' after paintings by Boucher, Lord Fife's set appears to have depicted scenes with 'Susanna, Joseph, Esther and Joshua'. The Coypel Tapestry, which was hung at Duff, may have been a 'sample' for a set depicting Don Quixote which were to prove as popular as the Boucher series, before Lord Fife chose a different set of subjects for his Great Room. The Fife House tapestries were sold on with the house after the death of the 2nd Earl.

This Private Drawing Room's transformation into a bedroom was achieved by swopping its contents with those of the South Western apartment and it seems to have been a bedroom from then on.

Above The Duke and Duchess of Fife with their Daughters

Below The Prince of Wales's Bedroom from *The Connoisseur*, September 1904

Closet off the Private Drawing Room

This room has been painted to reflect Jackson's 1814 scheme with black lines and stencilled corner-pieces on a blue ground (now simulated by paper). The fascination with black lining may be by association with Greek vase painting during the Greek Revival. In 1795 this room contained a group of prints on classical themes and prints of Charles I's children and the then current Prince of Wales on horseback. 'Two raised prints of birds' sound like the characteristic work of Dixon of Dublin and which must have been the survivors of the 'Twelve fine Jappan'd small Pictures, with the figures of Various Birds' which hung in the adjoining Drawing Room in 1761 and which also sound like Dixon's work through his characteristic japanned frames. Lord Fife may have acquired them in Dublin.

The Prince of Wales's Bedroom

This apartment was the finest in the house when first fitted up in the early 1760s after the very large family apartment occupied by Lord and Lady MacDuff and it is hardly surprising to find it occupied in the 1761 Inventory by his mother, the Countess of Fife, and thus presumably also by the Earl himself, when they visited their son and daughter-in-law. The importance of this room is underlined by its very splendid chimneypiece which frames a superb set of inlaid marble slips. The dado has a rich fret which is more Chinese than Grecian and it may be that this was deliberately chosen to complement the printed chintz textile furniture selected by the Countess. The mahogany bed, the curtains and chaircovers were all of 'printed cotton' but by 1795 this suite had been moved into Lady MacDuff's Dressing Room. The name 'The Countess of Fife's Bedroom' moved with it and the Red Damask Bed stood here. By 1809, however, when the house had taken on more and more of the air of a picture gallery, it was the 'South West Drawing Room' and contained much of the furniture from the Private Drawing room including the settee bed and the smaller family pictures.

By the time of the 4th Earl's sale in 1824 it was rechristened the 'Music Room' and had choice cabinet pictures including the reputed Velázquez of Charles I and 'Mary Queen of Scots With Her Infant Son. Painted on black Marble. This is an undoubted Original'. Attributed by the 2nd Earl to Holbein this was so precious it was retained by him at Fife House in London.

In 1883 this room became the Prince of Wales's Bedroom and it is recorded in a sketch of 1904. The bed must be one of the three 'French beds' described in the 1824 Sale Catalogue and is possibly that occupied by the 2nd Earl himself. It was not sold, and was apparently the richest, 'A superb French Mahogany Bed with Canopy, Drapery, and other ornaments fully mounted'. One of these beds had 'a superb Blue Satin Bed-cover richly embroidered with Gold said to have belonged to Napoleon Bonaparte'. The sketch also shows one of the sofa tables from Countess Agnes's North Drawing Room on the Second Floor and what may be a Louis XV style chair from Fife House in London, improved by Victorian deep springing. The mirror-faced doors, far from being added for the Prince's benefit, were probably repeated here for symmetry when they were installed in the Countess's Boudoir across the Vestibule in the late 1850s.

The white striped wallpaper repeats that found on the walls of this room when it became an Ancient Monument in 1953. The walls have always been papered and drips of green paint were visible behind the position of the original mid-Georgian doorheads when the room was being repapered in 1994.

Closet off the Prince of Wales's Bedroom

This retained its elegant black lining with anthemion corner pieces on a brilliant green ground by Jackson which had been protected by later papers. In 1761 the Countess's Closet had a ' Jappaned Buroe, wt. a Book Case above and Glass door' and a 'Dressing box Japand' again complementing the chintz next door. By 1843 : 'In a small closet, and not generally shown to visitors, is a coloured representation of Bonaparte, as he lay on the morning after his decease.'

The Family Apartment

The entire East side of the First Floor was occupied by Lord and Lady MacDuff as their family apartment. They shared the central bedroom on the East front but had each an entire bedroom apartment complete with Closet, stool room and Servant's Room in the mezzanine for their personal use and, by the standards of their time, this was luxurious. In June 1759 Lord MacDuff, shortly after his father had been created Earl of Fife , married Lady Dorothea Sinclair, the only child and heiress of the 9th Earl of Caithness. By May 1759, Dott wrote to Lord MacDuff to say that the family bedroom was almost finished but work was held up through the lack of chimney-marbles and, by the end of the month James Adam ' put a stop to every other thing in order to have it finished immediately'

The pressure from the approaching wedding day must have been intense. Sadly, the marriage was not to be a success. Lady Dorothea, known as Dolly to her family, was highly strung and sought relief at various spas. They seem to have led separate lives after 1769 with Lady Dorothea occupying Hermitage House on Leith Links near Edinburgh, where she died in 1818.

When the second floor rooms were completed after 1789, the Earl moved upstairs, but he may have previously occupied a room near the Library before then. The family apartment was put to alternative use. Lord and Lady Fife had no children, and the Nursery, so carefully planned by Adam beneath the family apartment in the basement, as at House of Dun, was never required.

ᢙ Lord MacDuff's ᢙ Dressing Room

In Adam's original scheme this dressing room was conveniently connected by the quadrant corridor with the vast library in the projected wing. As the outer of the two dressing rooms it would also have enabled him to interview visitors connected with the running of the estates without admitting them to the body of the house.

The architectural decoration is fairly simple and the compass-work fret is repeated on the dado and wooden chimneypiece with its deep red marble slips.

In the 1761 Inventory Lord MacDuff's Dressing room was fitted up in printed cotton including the 'tent bed' and the window curtains. Among a great deal else the adjoining closet contained two barometers, a small night table, a picture with a gilt frame, nineteen prints and three drawings. The chairs had blue and white check covers.

By 1795 the room had been transformed into the 'Blue Drawing Room' with gilt glasses over the chimney and between the windows. The room may have been painted 'Light French Gray' in oil over old wallpaper in 1794. Certainly, the room has always been papered and drips of blue were found behind the former position of the original doorframes when the room was redecorated in 1994. The room contained 22 portraits, several of which depicted the French Royal Family including Marie Antoinette, which Lord Fife had been able to obtain in the post-Revolutionary sales. In addition to more conventional drawing room furniture, there were 'six oak chairs' with 'Carpet bottoms' which would suggest that Lord Fife's antiquarianism had led him to collect, or preserve, a set of seventeenth-century Turkey work chairs suited in date to the room's early portraits.

By 1809 this was probably the drawing room in daily use because its contents now included a card table and the all important 'Tea Cadie with Fife Coronet'. By the time of the 1824 sale this room had grander contents but had also been the recipient of the 4th Earl's Spanish paintings which, on account of their rarity in Scotland, were a popular attraction: 'an Infant Jesus, with a crown of thorns, seated in a chair, from the school of Murillo; this painting, which is a general favourite with visitors, is said to have belonged to a monastery in Seville.' This room was also used to display the collection of miniatures which are recorded in an 1870s photograph; 'many of the miniatures, moreover, are richly set and framed, and display very curious, antique and tasteful workmanship'. In the Stranger's Guide, 1843, a further treasure was 'a sofa, the covering of which is said to have been worked by Queen Anne' while 'in the centre, stands a small neat table which was once the property of Garrick' suggesting that there may have been a continuing cult of antiquarian furniture in this room.

After 1857, Countess Agnes adopted this room as her boudoir and it was conveniently connected with the new family apartments on the second floor by the spiral stair. Her taste is recorded in an 1870s photograph, perhaps, taken as a memorial after her death . The marble bust is probably a portrait of her eldest daughter, Anne, Marchioness Townsend. The fringes on the chimney-shelf, bookcases and hanging shelves are especially characteristic of her taste. Her son, the first Duke, later adopted it as his business room but preserved his mother's decorations piously because it is described in 1904 'as still reflecting her taste, and was decorated to her order … in gold and green, and long mirrors richly gilt are hung upon the doors'. The mirrored doors, fitted dado bookcases and distinctive fringed trimming on the chimneypiece and bookshelves are all replicated in contemporary photographs of work by what must be the same firm at Cullen House and similar features survive at Castle Fraser.

ᴄᴏ Closet ᴄᴏ

In the 1807 catalogue this room contained portrait engravings presented to Lord Fife by their sitters including the Duchess of Northumberland and the Countess of Essex but the room had also something of the character of a cabinet of works by noble amateur artists including a view of Iona by the Earl of Buchan, the distinguished antiquary, and a view of Warwick Castle by Lady Louisa Greville, 'given to Lord Fife by herself'. The 'Press' in this Closet held, conveniently to hand, 'Tea things and some Derbyshire China tea things'. Both the Derby China and the Worcester teaset with a coronet and the initial 'F' had been listed in the China Room in 1795.

ᴄᴏ The Family Bed Chamber ᴄᴏ

In James Adam's letter of 31st May 1759 excusing the delay in sending marbles for this room he wrote that he was anxious 'give Your Lops a marble different from any, You have hitherto got, I Order'd a new block to be cut, which prevented it being got ready as soon as it wou'd otherwise …. The other chimney I am sure your Lop. will find extremely handsome, it is of purple marble'. In the 1761 Inventory this room was grandly fitted up to match the 'Mahogany Bed stead Complete, with rich blew water'd silk Curtains and blew Tammie Lynning wt. three Gilt Crowns fix'd on the Bed top and two pairs blue line and Tassels to do'. An easy chairs, six ordinary chairs and the curtains were all of the same silk. This luxury was completed with a 'fine Turkey bed Carpet'. To preserve the chaircovers there were slip cases described as 'check covers'.

By 1795 this finery had been cleared away and the bed was in store. The room was now known as the 'Striped Bed Chamber' from the 'silk and worsted' striped fabric it was now upholstered with. By the time of the 1824 Sale it had become 'The Hunting Room' but, having been identified as the obvious point of departure for Bryce's 1870 wing, it was partitioned to provide a linking passage and a Butler's pantry. After the removal of the wing the room was

Countess Agnes's Boudoir
*c.*1870

restored by Ancient Monuments in the 1970s and the cornice re-run.

This ignominious sub-division, however, was the means of preserving Jackson's highly decorative scheme of 1814 with a fictive sky above his shadowed fillets painted on the cove and it is possible that more of the coves were enlivened in this way. Knowing it was soon to be covered up the plasterer vaingloriously wrote his name in large letters by way of record 'Wm G Innes Plasterer Banff 1871' no less than three times. The partitioning also preserved a fragment of the original wallpaper with flowers and spiky leaves in green flock on a grey ground. Jackson wrote to Lord Fife that he 'was at a loss about the papering of the Bedrooms. As papering is an article rather out of line & of course cannot be so well done as when finished by professional men. What I would humbly suggest to your Losp. is that Mr Trotter of Princess Street Edinr. be employed to put up the paper & that his Manufacturers in London receive instructions to wait upon your Losp. with specimens of the paper'.

∽ Lady MacDuff's ∽ Dressing Room

In the 1761 Inventory Lady MacDuff's Dressing Room was fitted up in red printed cotton – possibly a decorative copper plate design – and included a 'resting bed' and a 'large press' for her clothes. The importance of this room was underlined was a 'large Pier Glass with a gilt frame', a draped dressing table 'of firr' with its 'toilet and scarff' draped round the tortoiseshell mirror, possibly placed below the pier glass.

By 1795, Lord Fife's mother's chintz suite had been moved into here and by 1824 it was the 'White Bedroom'. The original high wooden chimneypiece was replaced by a low marble chimneypiece.

∽ Lady MacDuff's Closet ∽

In the 1761 Inventory, as befitted the Closet of an important Lady, this room was furnished as a private retreat with:

Four Walnut-tree Chairs cover'd with printed Cotton
A fine Mahogany Secretaire, with a folding Table, cover'd with green Velvet, in the upper part of it eight drawers, with a looking Glass in the Middle of it, and in the drawers below the same, two Small mahogany Boxes, and four Brass handles, wt. Brass lock & Key, and below it a fine Mahogany Trea, all running on four brass Castors.
One Large looking Glass wt a white and Gilt Frame
One Grate finely polish'd, wt. Fender, Pocker, Tongs and Hearth Brush

The North Drawing Room
c.1870

One small Cupboard, with four images
One Book Case of Mahagony
One large Stool with a printed Cotton cover
One Small mahogany Table

⤙ *The Great Staircase* ⤚

It may seem strange that the Great Staircase was a void until the late 1780s, but there was no real need for it until the rooms on the State Floor came to be fitted out. The piano nobile remained a shell although the 3rd floor rooms were completed earlier. Duff House was in any case well supplied with staircases because the central service stair was augmented by the four spiral stairs in each corner.

Apart from a sense of completing unfinished business, Lord Fife's primary motivation in this final campaign was to display his ever expanding picture collection. Although there was a strong emphasis on economy, it is possibly also fair to say that with his metropolitan tastes, he was possibly attuned to then current fashionable taste for extreme simplicity in interior decoration. Nothing could be in greater contrast to the flamboyant effects that William Adam must have dreamed of in stucco and decorative painting for his state floor which would surely have eclipsed even such exuberance as Enzer's plasterwork in the Great Dining Room at Dun.

Lord Fife was anxious that the stair should be erected with minimum disturbance, and preferably when he was away, as he wrote in March 1791:
'I believe it will be best that Robinson delay everything about the stair till I am out of the country next winter, as I am sure it will keep … and I have the most horrid aversion to the least dirt.'

Robinson, his contractor, was therefore encouraged as far as possible to prefabricate the staircase and the individual steps seem to have come from the Hailes quarry near Edinburgh. The plasterwork was carried out by John Paterson, who seems to have had some difficulty in tuning in to the simplicity of his patron's taste. Although there was a stab at ornament in the Ionic columns which support the quarter landings on the ascent, the rail could hardly be plainer although its rectangular section, like the thinness of the steps themselves, gives an attenuated elegance to the whole. Lord Fife was keen that the rail be entrusted to a local man and wrote in September 1792:
'I have returned the estimate about the rail for the stair and you will get them to finish it as soon as possible I should be glad to see it up, I had rather give them my money than to a London workman so I hope on this principle they will finish it substantially.'

Stewart Souter, the local blacksmith, had also to

The North Drawing Room
*c.*1870

contend with 'altering the piece for the landing place' where he had to cope with the existing spirited panel, which perhaps had acted as a safety rail until the stair was finished, and he could not have effected this more simply than through the rather brutal superimposition. Although the marble pavement at the foot of the stair may appear uncharacteristically extravagant in all this simplicity, it was cut from a pre-existing supply in 1791. Lord Fife was doubtful as to 'whether I shall polish and lay the marble I have or lay the place in stone' but obviously plumped for marble in the end.

In William Adam's plan, there were to be three balancing doors at the upper landing the most Southerly of which would have led directly into the Salon and the two others into a rather dark lobby. Lord Fife attempted to introduce light to the dark lobby with a patent oval window as a borrow-light above the two lobby doors but the entire dividing wall was swept away in the late 1850s and the landing door to the Great Drawing Room suppressed.

The staircase was painted 'green and white' with 'mahogany colour' on the doors and the ceiling rose picked out in green on a white ground. The painter was keen to paint the rail green but Lord Fife demurred 'The rail of the stair cannot be green, it

may be grey' but seems to have allowed the ornamental panel at the stair head to be picked out in green.

The present scheme, however, is John Jackson's of 1814 with fictive mouldings and stencilled bands to offset the Second Earl's plainness (the fields and beds of the panels were repainted in 1994) an to modern eyes it seems engagingly naive, particularly in features like the painted vase in its niche between the windows. The stone steps were probably painted to look like white marble and the woodwork may have been grained. The 2nd Earl's simpler scheme was merely the background to the 34 pictures described in the 1807 Picture Catalogue some of which were very large indeed like the three copies after Rubens and Snyders from paintings in the Orlean's Collection and Frederick, Prince of Wales on horseback by Wooton. Incongruously among all the portraits was a 'Flower-piece Of Nun's Work Cut Paper'.

A sketch of the staircase in 1904 shows 'The large case of magnificent dessert service and vases of Dresden china, especially made for and presented to the Duke of Fife by the King of Saxony in 1882, when he had invested his Majesty with the order of the Garter – an embassy entrusted to him by our late Queen'.

Chimneypiece in the Great Drawing Room and detail of the Great Staircase
from *The Connoisseur*, October 1904

The Marble Lobby

From the style of the fitting up it must have been the Fifth Earl and his Countess who opened up the lobby and installed new doors and the plaster trusses to the stair opening. The new doorcases match those in the Countess's Boudoir.

The siena marbling must date from this time as well. This scheme only survived in the niche which had been covered over with the great gilt glass, now restored to the North Drawing Room. The full decorative scheme was restored by Tommy Hillocks and George Cruikshank from Buckie after research by the Stenhouse Conservation Centre. Like most 19th-century decorative painting it aims to deceive the eye through its geological faithfulness rather than at a loose decorative effect. The 'inlaid' geometric border is characteristic of the repertoire of D. R. Hay, the leading Decorator in Edinburgh who trained a generation of Scots' house painters. The original marbling is preserved in the niche which in 1904 'held a picturesque statue, a copy of the Venus di Medici (by Gian Bologna at Florence, produced for Prince Francesco de Medici) placed in a niche specially prepared for its reception. It is strange to say, the only full length piece of sculpture in Duff House'. The plasterwork of the cove and frieze was executed for the 2nd Earl.

The Great Drawing Room

This is breath-taking in its austerity and as a contrast with the Baroque exterior. Adam's 'Salon' or Great Dining Room had been intended as a 'cube of thirty feet' but in August 1790 Lord Fife wrote 'I intend to make the present Cube just 25 feet in height'. In William Adam's design the central rooms had flues in both their West and East Walls for paired chimneypieces and considerable energy had to be expended in removing the Western chimney-breasts in 1791. Paterson's plasterwork was to be drastically simplified by omitting the ornaments in the frieze and similarly the woodwork was intended to have composition enrichments sent up from London but these too were omitted leaving only the central rose with its fan patera, rinceau and eagles framed by narrow bands of husks.

In 1794 the walls were painted 'fine green dead in oil' directly on to the plaster with 'best Dead white 4 coats' on the woodwork. The 'ornament in Centre of Drawing Room ceiling 2 coats in oil and finished Distemper Colours'. The chimneypiece with composition enrichments is a pair to that in the North Drawing Room and was sent up from London. Its maker is not known.

From the 1795 and even the 1809 Inventories there is no great conviction that this room was ever convincingly fitted up as a Drawing Room. There were certainly both chimney and pier-glasses in gilt frames and a gilt lustre suspended from the ceiling. In 1795 two card tables stood under the pier glasses but the only seat furniture was a set of fifteen and two elbow chairs in 'black and white Japand … with wicker bottoms' but by 1809 these had been replaced by 'twelve mahogany back stool Chairs with worsted Crimson Damask with pink covers'. In 1796 the Earl bought two 'India commode Tables with oil cloth covers', one of which was a little higher than the other and had to be altered , to replace the card tables.

The real point of the room had always been to display the portraits which numbered 37 in the 1807 picture Catalogue and had a distinct theme spanning the Kings and Queens of England from Henry V to George III and the Catalogue supplied biographical data as of Elizabeth I:

'Was a woman of Learning and extraordinary Understanding. She completed the Reformation by her Art and Address …. What executions were in her Reign, were legal, that of Mary, Queen of Scots, excepted …'

The 4th Earl may have left this show-piece untouched and after his grand furniture departed in 1824, it seems to have had even more of a museum and gallery air through the addition of 'several antique vessels for the holding of Holy water, belonging at one time, we presume to religious houses' and an array of taxidermy including stuffed specimens of Capercailzie, the Norwegian Grouse imported by the Fourth Earl from Norway and a 'real Highland Wild Cat from Mar Lodge'.

Countess Agnes improved this room by the addition of composition ornaments including the swags on the doors and Adamesque doorheads.

Regrettably these overdoors were removed in 1993. The walls were described in 1904 as being in 'ecru [the colour of unbleached linen] with mouldings and ornaments in white bas relief whilst hangings of gold brocade afford a deep toned setting for

the lighter shades used in the wall decoration'. These painted ornaments sound like Jackson's work. The japanned commodes had been replaced by fancier ones described as 'two Adam commodes in white and gold, with plaques of Wedgwood china, whilst the French plates in the centre of the doors appear as if added at a later period'. By this date the pictures had been edited and diversified with an eye to quality of artist rather than rank of sitter and there had been an influx of the Spanish pictures.

During restoration in 1993, when the hotel's panels and the remains of the raspberry moire paper were removed, the 2nd Earl's paintwork was discovered intact and the author recalls the excitement as it was suddenly realised that the 2nd Earl's picture hang survived through differential fading on the North wall. There had been five full-lengths across the wall opposite the windows, above the height of the door, with a large picture flanked by smaller portraits on either side of the door. A more faintly faded patch showed up on the right in the lower register where a picture had been substituted.

The chimneypiece had been sold before the house was preserved as an Ancient Monument. It was traced by John Knight, the Ancient Monuments' Supervising Architect, to a storeroom in Aberdeen University. Miraculously it had survived fire damage to its packing case and, after restoration, it was returned to the house. The parquet floor was installed by the hotel.

✆ The North Drawing Room ✆

This was fitted up by the Second Earl at the same time as the Great Drawing Room but nominally functioned as a Dining Room. In Adam's scheme this would have been the single Great Drawing Room with the State Bedroom and the second best bedroom apartment leading from it. This room is much richer than the Great Drawing Room with swags of husks in the frieze and an elaborate rose surrounded by swags enclosing vases and shields. In 1807 the portraits in this room were predominately of the sixteenth and seventeenth centuries giving it the air of a National Portrait Gallery.

The 1795 and 1809 Inventories show that this room was more or less fitted up as a Dining Room and the pier tables from the Dining Room below were certainly moved up here but the lack of other dining furniture suggests that again it was really purely a picture gallery with no practical function. By 1824 it had grander Drawing Room furniture but the 2nd Earl's pictures were still in place and particular attention in 1843 was directed to the floor 'of pine from Mar Lodge', which was admired for its excellence. This room was redecorated by Countess Agnes after 1857 and is recorded in two 1870s photographs (see pages 56 & 57). Her determination to transform at least one room with a complete suite of modern furniture reflects the unusual history of this house which had lacked a Countess's touch for almost a century and thus she must have felt a particular desire to impose a more feminine character. The Countess's early death must, in turn, have led to a desire to preserve her taste at Duff. This room's memorial quality was underlined by the dominance of the Countess's portrait of 1863 by Sir Francis Grant, 'presented by a grateful tenantry' while its pair, depicting the Earl, was hung in the Dining Room below. Her decorations survived until 1904 when this room was described thus:

'the ante-drawing-room reflects the individual taste of Agnes, late Countess of Fife, and is hung with decided colours. Adam's gilt furniture is upholstered in royal blue and ecru, whilst the velvet curtains over the windows and portières are of the same hue.'

The Countess must have added the papier mâché enrichments to the corners of the ceiling. The two 1870s photographs show that in spite of the Countess's efforts, her effects for all their elaboration still play second fiddle to the 2nd Earl's portrait gallery. It must have been an important opportunity for her cabinet-maker to shine and they have risen to the occasion with a flurry of over-elaboration. Of her furnishings only the over-mantel mirror survives above the chimney and has never left the house.

✆ The Second Floor Bedrooms ✆

Because of the abundance of back stairs, the 2nd Earl was able to make a start on the Second floor bedrooms before the Great Staircase was completed in 1792. Like the Great and North Drawing Rooms they were fitted up in an exceptionally plain manner with simple painted walls and elegantly pared-down joinery. The two Southern bedroom apartments were nominally fitted up as Drawing Rooms at the time of the 1807 Picture Catalogue but they must have

Opposite Detail of the chimneypiece in the Great Drawing Room

functioned as yet more picture rooms.

The 5th Earl and Countess Agnes adopted the Eastern rooms on the Second floor as their own suite and it was probably the Countess who installed the rather florid Louis XV Revival chimneypiece in black and gold marble in her Dressing Room. These rooms were also used by the Duke and Duchess of Fife. Their daughters had a framed fragment of the 'tartan plaid given to Bonnie Prince Charlie by Lady Mackintosh of Moy' hanging in their apartment.

During restoration work, the shadow of the 2nd Earl's picture hang was also found on a green ground on the wall opposite the windows in the South East bedroom apartment. The South west Bedroom was fitted up as a Sitting Room for the Prince of Wales in 1883 and was conveniently connected by the spiral stair with his bedroom below.

The Third Floor

The Library had lost much of its character through being cut up into hotel bedrooms and has now been converted into the Education Suite. However, two of Dott's presses with their 'Chinese doors' survive at the entrance. The handsome Gothic Revival chimneypiece in veined white marble in the Southern compartment was probably originally installed in the Parlour on the Ground Floor and is a reminder of that room's former elegance.

The North West Turret was the Armoury and some of its former contents are now on display in Banff Museum. The South West Turret may have been used temporarily by Lord Fife as his Bedroom and it retained remnants of a handsome wallpaper with sprays of pink carnations and white flowers against a blue ground. Lord Fife migrated round the Upper Floor as his building works proceeded. The Eastern Rooms on the Third Floor were fitted up in the late 1750s and are similar in character to the First Floor rooms with compass-fret chair rails and some engagingly provincial joinery. The chimneypiece in the South East Closet retained a few of its deep purple manganese tiles depicting vases of flowers.

The Ground Floor

Although this was plainly finished as domestic offices, there were some refinements on this floor.

Banff and the River Deveron
by John Fleming, *c.*1825

The Bridge of Alvah
by Charles Cordiner

The Muniment Room in the South West Closet retains its solid iron door and lock-case and was vaulted to render it fireproof. Perhaps because the Second Floor took so long to finish the centre room on the North front was refitted as the 'Parlour' to provide an informal Dining Room for the family when there were no guests. Among the many pictures hanging here in the 1807 Picture Catalogue were two views of Fife House in London by Tomkins and a portrait of 'A favourite Dog (Called Dick) with a view of the Surrey Side of the River Thames, opposite to the Garden of Fife House', also by Tomkins.

⌒ The Park and Garden ⌒

From the outset, the design of the gardens must have been a prime consideration in the choice of a site for the house and so it is not surprising to find an entry in William Adam's accounts of 1741 for supplying 'a plan of the whole grounds about the house'. During the 1730s a formal lay-out would have been desired and the flat bed of the valley of the Deveron River just as it entered Banff Bay would have been suitable for the creation of elaborate parterres. The house had sufficient distance from the town while being close enough to dominate through its impressive silhouette. Unfortunately Adam's design does not survive and the dispute about the building of the house

meant that little was done to create an appropriate setting. Adam also charged for designs for a 'Mausoleum with a Temple in the Island' but only the latter was executed. It was thus left to the 2nd Earl to develop the Park. During this hiatus there had been a radical change in taste in favour of a more naturalistic style in the manner of 'Capability Brown'. The Deveron was to be the key to the evolution of a design in which a two mile stretch of the river valley was to be landscaped and the house was set off by green parkland diversified by clumps of trees.

Near the town, the dominance of the house was manifest in the way in which the bridge was lined up with the main drive to the house. Sadly modern road improvements have blurred this design but one of the original pair of lodges at the East end of the bridge survives, although rebuilt. Like most Scottish houses, Duff also had a walled garden combining a Kitchen garden with fruit and flowers and part of this still survives to the North of the new roadway from the Bridge into Banff. Now known as the Princess Royal Park this is cared for by the District Council. The Lodge, which guarded the drive Southwards to the house, is now the Tourist Information office. This avenue leading to the house, which still survives, passes the offices on its left which are now part of the Duff Royal Golf Club. If these features are conventional enough, what was to make the landscape at Duff remarkable was the way in which the more rugged scenery upstream, where the valley narrows in a deep gorge, was to be embraced into the overall design. In 1772, Lord Fife had the majestic arched Alvah Bridge constructed across this narrow chasm. This dramatic passage of the landscape with its rocky crags and deep pools was soon established as a local beauty spot. The two bridges thus became the limits of a circuit of drives down the banks of the Deveron enjoying, in a compact compass, a surprising diversity of scenery. Unfortunately, no designs for this landscaping survive which was to be further improved with the benefit of professional advice from Thomas White.

The Park is now divided up among a variety of different users with much of the area nearest to the house landscaped into the Duff Royal Golf Course. If it has lost its overall clarity, most of its features survive, particularly the large number of eye-catchers on the horizon. The Temple of Venus to the East, above the town of MacDuff, is perhaps the most strikingly sited. Approached by a gentle path from the bridge, it provides an excellent vantage point for the appreciation of the broad sweep of the Park. Across on the West bank the Dovecot was originally topped by the shaft of the Old Banff Market Cross and further down the Deveron there were yet more temples on the skyline defining the limits of the Park.

An impression of the former charms of the Park is readily gained by following the drive along the West bank of the Deveron which originally led to the Bridge of Alvah. This passes between gatepiers topped by vases decorated with flowers and fruit and although the drive is now thickly wooded it soon becomes obvious that the drive is along a terrace with views down to the river below. In Spring this walk is thickly carpeted with snowdrops. The drive passes the icehouse which was restored by Banff and Buchan District Council in 1980 and then leads on to the 2nd Earl of Fife's Mausoleum which was built from 1793 to receive the mortal remains of the Duff dynasty. In his choice of a Gothic style, Lord Fife followed his antiquarian taste but he must also have been anxious to recall not only the ancient burial ground of the nearby Carmelite Monastery but also the antiquity of the Duff family. The Mausoleum was restored by Banff and Buchan District Council in 1980 but had sadly lost a certain amount of its original character including its painted glass and the statues of Faith and Hope that guarded its entrance. Much of its Gothic ornament was made of an up-to-the-minute material, Coade Stone. Lord Fife's antiquarian effect went beyond his choice of the Gothic style because he collected monuments of his chosen ancestors from several local churches which were incorporated into the overall design to proclaim the length of the Duffs' pedigree.

From the main drive paths branch off to thread their way up and down the river bank and although often overgrown in places there is still a powerful sense of the Park's former beauties.

Stuffed stag's head shot in Duff House Park 1797,
now at Mar Lodge